P9-DNU-680

finding
JEFFERSON

BOOKS BY ALAN DERSHOWITZ

Blasphemy: How the Religious Right Is Hijacking
Our Declaration of Independence
Preemption: A Knife That Cuts Both Ways
What Israel Means to Me
Rights from Wrongs: A Secular Theory
of the Origins of Rights
America on Trial
The Case for Peace
The Case for Israel
America Declares Independence
Why Terrorism Works
Shouting Fire
Letters to a Young Lawyer
Supreme Injustice
Genesis of Justice
Just Revenge
Sexual McCarthyism
The Vanishing American Jew
Reasonable Doubts
The Abuse Excuse
The Advocate's Devil
Contrary to Popular Opinion
Chutzpah
Taking Liberties
Reversal of Fortune
Best Defense
Criminal Law: Theory and Process
Psychoanalysis: Psychiatry and Law

finding
JEFFERSON

A Lost Letter, a Remarkable Discovery, and the First Amendment in an Age of Terrorism

ALAN DERSHOWITZ

BICENTENNIAL
1807
WILEY
2007
BICENTENNIAL

John Wiley & Sons, Inc.

342.73
D438f

This book is printed on acid-free paper. ∞

Published by John Wiley & Sons, Inc., Hoboken, New Jersey
Published simultaneously in Canada

Photo credits: page 8, Suzanne Kreiter for the *Boston Globe*; pages 10, 11, 15, 17, 23, 80, Alan Dershowitz; pages 21, 22, 24, Tom Ashe; page 52, Metropolitan Museum of Art; page 196, courtesy Library of Congress

Wiley Bicentennial Logo: Richard J. Pacifico

Design and composition by Navta Associates, Inc.

For general information about our other products and services, please contact our Customer Care Department within the United States at (800) 762-2974, outside the United States at (317) 572-3993 or fax (317) 572-4002.

Wiley also publishes its books in a variety of electronic formats. Some content that appears in print may not be available in electronic books. For more information about Wiley products, visit our web site at www.wiley.com.

ISBN 978-0-470-16711-3

Printed in the United States of America

10 9 8 7 6 5 4 3 2 1

Dedicated to my fellow flea-market mavens, used-book-store stalkers, compulsive collectors, and eBay addicts. May you never pass up the perfect tchotchke. Jefferson could have been describing frustrated collectors who passed up good acquisitions when he cautioned his nephew about frustrated travelers:

> Their eyes are forever turned back to the object they have lost and its recollection poisons the residue of their lives. Their first and most delicate passions are hackneyed on unworthy object here, and they carry home with the dregs, insufficient to make themselves or anybody else happy.

May you always come home with worthy objects.

This book is also dedicated to my history professor, John Hope Franklin, who brought American history alive by teaching it, writing it, and living it.

CONTENTS

ACKNOWLEDGMENTS

I found the Jefferson letter on Friday, September 8, 2006, and by Monday, September 11, 2006, I had written nearly ten thousand words of this book. For me, writing, collecting, and Jefferson are powerful compulsions. Writing *about* finding Jefferson became a supercompulsion. But even compulsive writers need help.

I was assisted in the research by Peter Mulcahy, Charles Johnson, and Michael Sugar. My agent, Helen Rees, and my editor, Hana Lane, turned my compulsion into this book. My family members, who tolerate my compulsions, provided the usual doses of encouragement and constructive criticism. My friends, including Roland Savage, read the manuscript and offered suggestions.

My most profound thanks goes to Thomas Jefferson for preserving his brilliant ideas in letters and for understanding that these letters, if preserved for history, provide a unique insight into a complex mind that helped found our great nation.

PART

I

———⟩●⟨———

THE
COLLECTOR
AND HIS
PASSIONS

1

My Passion for Collecting

I'm a collector. I've always been a collector. As a kid I collected Brooklyn Dodger autographs, baseball cards, comic books, stamps, coins, bottle tops, and anything else that could fit into one drawer in the bureau I shared with my younger brother (and even some things that couldn't, like tropical fish). I never threw anything away (except the dead fish), much to my mother's chagrin.

"What are you gonna do with all that junk?" she asked imploringly.

"It's gonna be valuable someday," I responded, pointing with pride to my neatly organized treasures.

And they would have been valuable someday—at least, the comic books and the baseball cards—had my mother not thrown them out the minute I left home for law school (I lived at home while attending Brooklyn College). I once found a T-shirt that well summarized my plight (and that of an entire generation of young collectors). It said, "Once I was a millionaire . . . then my mother threw my baseball cards away."

My mother, who was a frugal survivor of the Great Depression, didn't throw away my stamps or coins. Those she gave to my brother and younger cousins, who kept them until they left home, when these collections were promptly recycled to yet younger relatives. Because I was the oldest among my more than thirty first cousins, the recycling went only one way, with me being the involuntary recycler and never the recyclee of any good stuff. Where my treasures are now, no one knows, and I suspect that the statute of limitations has long since passed on any repleven action (a lawsuit for return of property) I might have had against cousin Norman. The comic books, the baseball cards, and the autographs my mother simply threw into the garbage, because—unlike the stamps and the coins, which were currency—they had no intrinsic value. The remainder of my tchotchkes (Yiddish for inexpensive collectibles) went to some deserving neighborhood kid or to tchotchke heaven. All I know is I never saw them again.

Nor did I really care. After all, I was going to law school—Yale, to boot. (My mother never forgave me for turning down Harvard. For years she told people, "He got into Harvard, but he went to Yale.") I was on to bigger and better things. The Dodgers had abandoned Brooklyn for Los Angeles, and I had abandoned baseball (at least until I moved to Boston and joined "Red Sox Nation"). Who needed comic books when I could read Blackstone's *Commentaries on the Law?*

My penchant for collecting didn't abandon me, however. It just went in a different direction. I'd managed to find three volumes of an early American edition of Blackstone. (I'm still looking for the fourth to complete my set—the 1791 edition. If anyone has it for sale, please be in touch.) I started to collect autographs of Supreme Court Justices, Vanity Fair prints, and old books. I have found first editions of books by Lewis Carroll, Theodore Herzl, Anne Frank, and others. When I became a full professor at Harvard in 1967 (that's when my mother finally stopped complaining that I had chosen Yale), Professor Henry Hart gave me an original copy of the complete transcript of the Sacco-Vanzetti trial that had been owned by Felix Frankfurter—who had been one of the lawyers in the case—and had been given to him by Frankfurter when Hart became a professor. These volumes are part of a large collection of historic trial transcripts, many from England, that I have accumulated over the years.

I also collected old newspapers with contemporaneous accounts of significant historical events, such as the assassination of Lincoln, the death of Hitler, the establishment of Israel, and the duel between Alexander Hamilton and Aaron Burr. It was fascinating to read how these events were reported at the time. It helped me to better understand why journalism is called "the first draft of history." When Harvard Law School put its vast newspaper collection on microfilm, I bought several volumes of old editions of the *New York Times*. The ads are an especially interesting window to the past.

I did not have much money when I was young, so I was always searching for bargains. I went to the used book stores that lined Fourth Avenue in Manhattan and to flea markets, garage sales, library de-acquisitions, and junk shops. This was before eBay, *Antiques Roadshow*, and magazines dedicated to the art of collecting. To me, collecting was not an art; it was an addiction.

"What are you looking for?" my friends asked. "What do you expect to find—the original Declaration of Independence?"

"No," I assured them, knowingly. "The original is in the Archives. But an early copy?"

There is an urban myth—maybe even a true story, who knows?—of someone who found an early copy of the Declaration in an old frame behind a print of dogs playing poker that he had bought for five bucks at a flea market. He sold it for a fortune. I have never sold anything. For me, collecting is a one-way street. I *collect*. I don't *distribute*. I also look behind every print I buy. So far, no luck. The best I've come up with are some interesting old newspapers—one that announced Hitler's death. But I did manage to find a beautiful nineteenth-century facsimile of the Declaration that hangs behind my desk in my home office.

My wife, Carolyn, who is the opposite of a collector, is known in the family as "Swoop," because she throws away anything that's not bolted to the ground. Opposites do attract. Carolyn tolerates my passion for collecting as long as I keep my stuff in my home office, which is overflowing with tchotchkes, books, old newspapers, art, and antiques. She is thinking about imposing a new rule: for every new purchase, I have to get rid of something of equal size. I can't. I won't! Off-site storage seems like a reasonable compromise.

My wife and I do share a passion for collecting real antiques and art. In general, we have to agree on an object before we buy it, but we each have the right to buy art for our own home offices, based on our individual tastes. Several years ago, my wife and I were in Los Angeles visiting my son, Elon, who is a film producer. As usual, I was looking for antiques and my wife was exploring one of her many passions—shoes. I walked down Melrose Avenue and saw a store with old amusement park gizmos on the sidewalk. (We have an old Coney Island bumper car in our living room.) When I went in, my eyes were drawn immediately to the rear third of an old Cadillac from the late fifties—you know, the ones with the enormous fins and shiny chrome. Some enterprising artist had turned it into a couch, with the trunk as the seating area. It was beautiful.

It was also nostalgic, reminding me of my teenage years, when I and several friends chipped in to buy an old Caddy that barely worked. It went a mile on two gallons. Our interest was not in a driving machine, however, but in a place to make out with our girlfriends. We were more interested in the backseat than in the front. We made up for the cost of the car by renting out the backseat to friends. (Fortunately, nobody ever got beyond second base, so we could not be charged with operating a house—or a car—of ill repute.)

The Cadillac for sale on Melrose Avenue was a lot nicer and shinier than our beat-up old one, but it still evoked fond memories. I had to have it. But would my wife approve? I couldn't find her, and the salesman warned me that there had been a lot of interest in the car-sofa. So I bought it, rationalizing the decision by thinking that I could always shoehorn it into my home office. To my delight, Carolyn loved it as much as I did, though she pleaded the Fifth to my rigorous cross-examination about *her* teenage experiences in the backseats of cars. The Cadillac now sits proudly in our living room (next to the bumper car) and has frequently been photographed for magazine spreads about our home.

This photograph appeared in a Boston Globe *article about my collections ("Inside This Crusty Lawyer Is a Warm and Cuddly Collector," July 24, 2003). My wife, Carolyn—aka Swoop—is a good sport when it comes to my collecting. To my delight, she loved the Cadillac sofa pictured here at right as much as I did.*

Carolyn and I do not always agree, however, about my large acquisitions. Following the Cadillac coup, I became overconfident and bid at an auction on an enormous painting by the mid-twentieth-century French-Jewish artist Mané-Katz. It shows a young Talmud student trying to study a sacred text but becoming distracted by the image of a voluptuous nude woman hovering over him. That was me in elementary school, and I thought Carolyn, who loves art from that period, would share my enthusiasm. Boy, was I wrong. She hates its "cartoonish" look, and she isn't crazy about the theme. So into my office it went, on a back wall where Carolyn doesn't have to look at it when she pops in to say hello. (If anyone is interested in buying the Mané-Katz, I suggest that you call my wife when I'm not home. She might offer you a really great deal!)

I never thought I could afford to collect great art, since I had always lived on a budget. But I bought my first piece of real art for $25 in 1965, when I was a twenty-six-year-old assistant professor. I was sent on an all-expenses-paid trip to Paris by the dean of the law school. His pretense was that he wanted me to look at schools of criminology, but I have always suspected that he really wanted to expose me to European culture, since I was probably the only Harvard faculty member who had never traveled abroad. Although I still spoke with a Brooklyn accent and certainly didn't exude culture, I had always loved classical music and opera (as evidenced by the fact—for which my wife and kids have never forgiven me—that I turned down a chance to see the Beatles in concert during my Paris trip and instead went to a mediocre performance of *Rigoletto* at the Paris Opera House, where the Chagall paintings on the ceiling were better than the singing on the stage). I also have always loved art and spent considerable amounts of time in museums—once for a sustained period of time when I was suspended from high school for throwing a dummy of myself off the roof. (I tell the full story in my book *The Best Defense*, on page 12.)

While in Paris, I went to a number of art galleries. At one of them I saw a Kandinsky lithograph with which I immediately fell in love (see the illustration on page 10). The asking price was the equivalent of $50 (the franc was quite weak then), but I bargained the owner down to $25. It still hangs proudly in our home and was recently appraised for considerably more than I paid. (So what? I'm never going to sell it!) In Paris I also bought an oil painting by a Lithuanian artist named Vytautas Kasiulis, who I thought would be the next Picasso. It, too, hangs in obscurity in my home office. I paid an immense sum for it—at least by 1965 standards: $200. It's now worth at least half that.

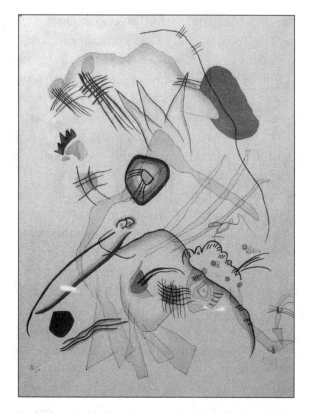

*I purchased this Kandinsky lithograph during a trip
to France when I was twenty-six—an all-expenses-
paid mission by the dean of Harvard Law to get me
a little "cultcha." It was a good find at only $25;
since then, good finds in my collection have been
known as "Kandinskies."*

The Kandinsky purchase was the first of many. Some
turned out to be what we refer to in my family as
"Kandinskies"—bargains that became far more valuable.
Others turned out to be "Kasiulises." Not all of our art is
great, but each piece reminds us of something we experienced. I'm reminded of the bon mot by the director of a

French museum, "Certainly we have bad paintings, [but we] have only the 'greatest' bad paintings." I have at least one "bad" drawing; it is a signed series of sketches of faces drawn by Picasso on the back of a French menu. I suspect he paid the bill—39 francs—with the drawing. Today we own more than a hundred pieces of art—none very valuable, but most of them fine works that we treasure. (Because of their sentimental value to us, we have a top-of-the-line security system to

This painting, by a more or less unknown Lithuanian artist named Vytautas Kasiulis, was less of a find than the Kandinsky and less of a bargain. Inauspicious purchases are thus known as "Kasiulises."

protect them, so don't get any ideas!) Some of our art now hangs in the homes of my children, which gives us great pleasure.

Over the years I have found a watercolor by the late-nineteenth-century impressionist Paul Signac in an old frame at a flea market (I paid $75 for it), an early pen and ink Rockwell Kent drawing at a book fair, a Dalí lithograph in a California junk store, and an alleged drawing by Egon Schiele in a rural French flea market. The Schiele is probably a fake or a student drawing (I paid $50), but I also have a real Schiele, which I bought at an auction (for considerably more). We own four related pieces of art—all bought separately—by four Jewish artists who lived in the same house in Montmartre during the second decade of the twentieth century. When we purchased them, we were not aware of the connection. The first is a painting (a self-portrait) by Chaim Soutine, the second a drawing by Amedeo Modigliani, the third a painting by Mose Keisling, and the fourth a sculpture by Ossip Zadkine. Although their styles are quite different, they were called the "emotional school," probably as the result of some Jewish stereotype. After we learned of the connection, we bought a drawing of Soutine by Modigliani. Keisling was also sketched by Modigliani, but I was outbid for it at a recent auction.

I always buy items of Judaica that I come across in Germany, Poland, and other European countries, since I consider it almost a sacred obligation to liberate these remnants of the Holocaust and return them to Jewish hands. I intend to donate the ones that my family doesn't want to keep to Jewish museums. Once, on a visit to Munich, I saw in an antique shop window a Jewish pocket watch with Hebrew numerals and the words Shana Tova (a good new year) engraved on the back. When I bought it, the store owner asked me in broken English whether I was interested in "more items like that." Thinking that he was referring to Jewish items, I said yes. He then took me to a back room and retrieved a box from the closet. He opened it and showed me dozens of items of Nazi memorabilia, some with Jewish stars—armbands, ID cards, and the like. This is what he meant by "items like that." Nazi memorabilia cannot be sold or displayed openly in Germany, so he kept these objects in the back room, displaying only the "Jewish" items. I bought a small doll of Hitler with a movable arm that performed the "Führer salute." I wanted people to see what some Germans are still buying. I display it in a corner, facing an American World War II Hitler doll whose large rear end is a pincushion. If only voodoo had worked!

I have a considerable collection of old and not-so-old anti-Semitic posters and hotel ads that exclude Jews, but my prized possession within this genre is an actual blood libel leaflet from Nuremberg dated 1492 that portrays a Jew "bleeding" a Christian child for Passover matzoh. It calls for revenge against the Jews.

I have a large collection of Yiddish postcards—particularly, New Year's cards from the late nineteenth and early twentieth centuries. Many are remarkably secular, featuring new inventions like the airplane, the phonograph, and the radio. I also collect photographs, drawings, and books relating to the French trial, conviction, and ultimate vindication of Alfred Dreyfus. I have a prayer book from the Polish city of Przemysl, where my grandfather once lived. It was published there on the eve of the Holocaust and managed to survive, though its owners almost certainly did not. It has a wine stain on the page with the Kiddush (the blessing over wine). I often think of the child, now long gone, who spilled the wine while making Kiddush, as I intone the same prayer seventy years later. When I visited the city of Przemysl in the 1990s, the official who showed us around denied that a Jewish community had ever been there. I sent him a Xerox of the first page of the prayer book showing that it had been published by a Jewish publishing house in Przemysl in 1936.

I used to own a valuable collection of "Responsa" volumes by eminent Jewish legal scholars dating back to the sixteenth century. These books contained legal opinions given in response to questions put by members of the community on the widest range of religious and secular issues. They constituted the "common law" of the Jewish people. Recently, I donated my collection to the Harvard Law School. I kept one volume of responses from the Holocaust written by Rabbi Ephraim Oshry.

My Judaica collection includes a remarkable Marrano chalice with a fascinating history. When the Jews of Spain were required, on pain of death, to convert to Catholicism, many merely pretended to do so but secretly continued to practice Judaism. The converts were called "Marranos," which means "pigs," and those who continued to practice Judaism were called "crypto-Jews." From the outside, the Marrano chalice appears to be an ordinary silver decorative object, but when it is taken apart, it contains secret compartments that hide Jewish religious objects, such as a scroll of Esther, Sabbath and Chanukah candelabras, a mezuzah, a Kiddush cup, and a spice box. It tells an important story of Jewish persecution and resilience. It is among my most prized possessions, and it became a "character" in one of my novels (*Just Revenge*, published in 1999). I lend it out to schools to bring alive the history of the Inquisition.

In 1989, my wife and I spent the Passover holiday in Egypt, where we attended one of the last seders in the home of an old Jewish-Egyptian family in Cairo, which is now

A Marrano chalice from my collection of Judaica. I love pieces with an interesting history. This chalice was used by Jews who were forced to convert to Catholicism during the Inquisition. On the outside it appears ordinary, but within it contains secret compartments for hiding Jewish religious objects.

without a significant Jewish presence. The next day we were taken by our Muslim guide to the Jewish cemetery, where the caretaker sent his grandson into a small cave in which the Jews of Egypt—there had been a large Jewish population until 1967—had buried their sacred books. It is called a *geniza*. (This was not *the* famous *geniza* discovered a century ago, but a smaller, more local one.) He came out of the cave carrying some old scrolls and books. He showed them to us and was about to toss them into the trash bin. I asked whether I could have them. He gave them to me, and I stuffed them into my pockets and Carolyn's handbag.

When we got back to our hotel and could inspect them, they turned out to include some real treasures: the first part of a seventeenth-century Torah scroll, an old Passover

Haggadah, a cardboard sign from the front of a synagogue, and an invitation to a Hebrew concert during World War I. When my daughter was bat mitzvahed fourteen years later, we presented her with the framed Torah fragment since it contained the Torah portion she read in the synagogue.

I also collect antiquities, ranging from Canaanite idols to Greek, Roman, and Etruscan statuary. (I am fortunate that an old friend from Cambridge, whose family owned a wonderful antiquities shop on Brattle Street—which became Burdick's Chocolates, so I can't complain—is now in charge of antiquities at one of the major auction houses.) One of my favorite antiquities is a four-thousand-year-old Syrian mold from which multiple gods—talk about polytheism—could be shaped out of clay. Another is a three-thousand-year-old erotic sculpture—from the Arabian Peninsula—of a couple engaged in an exotic form of sexual intercourse. Such a sculpture produced in today's Saudi Arabia would result in an exotic form of punishment.

Several years ago, I represented a British antiquities dealer who was accused of peddling fakes. He offered to pay me in—you guessed it—antiquities, which he insisted were real. Although we eventually won the case, I still demanded to be paid with money. ("Would you want to be represented by a lawyer who would accept payment in antiquities from a client who was accused of selling fakes?" I asked him rhetorically.) He did, however, give me an antiquity as a bonus. I checked it out. (I had to, because I needed to pay tax on its value.) It's real.

I have a stone facade from a first-century synagogue, an Egyptian sarcophagus, a Roman mosaic, an Etruscan head, a pre-Columbian sculpture of a "Thinker," and a Byzantine cross. One of my Orthodox uncles was appalled by my placement of Jewish religious objects in close proximity to

Christian, Muslim, and heathen objects, but my placement decisions are made on aesthetic, not religious, grounds. For example, the ancient sarcophagus hangs opposite a brightly colored contemporary "sarcophagus" by Keith Haring.

One of my favorite antiquities, because it deals with the law, is a nearly four-thousand-year-old "building cone" from Sumer. It contains an inscription by King Lipit-Estar, who wrote one of the earliest legal codes in history, which was a source for the Code of Hammurabi and the Bible. The inscription reads as follows:

> I, Lipit-Estar, humble shepherd of Nippur, true farmer of Ur, unceasing provider for Eridu, [a] priest fit for Urek, king of Isin, king of the land of Sumer and Akkad, favourite of the goddess Inanna, when I established justice in the land of Sumer and Akkad, I built the "House of Justice" by the irrigation canal, the pre-eminent place of the gods.

Objects that relate to the law, in particular, have a special attraction for me. This four-thousand-year-old Sumerian building cone contains an inscription by King Lipit-Estar, who wrote one of the earliest legal codes in history, which was a source for the Code of Hammurabi and the Bible.

I love objects that are both aesthetically beautiful and historically meaningful. My bias is toward objects that have a personal significance to me as a lawyer, as an American, as a Jew, and as an academic.

I have documents signed by Presidents James Madison, James Monroe, and Andrew Jackson, as well as by Henry Clay and Aaron Burr. I also have personal letters from modern presidents—Gerald Ford, Jimmy Carter, Bill Clinton, and George W. Bush, as well as an autograph collection of every president of the United States (including, I hope, the next one!).

The joy of collecting lies generally in finding an item that appeals to the collector's aesthetic, historical, or personal sensibilities. Finding the object is an end unto itself: holding in one's hand a piece of the original Dead Sea Scrolls (which I was allowed to do in the vaults of the Rockefeller Museum in Jerusalem), beholding the signature of one of the collector's heroes, and touching the piece of paper on which this person wrote. But the joy is magnified when the item has a value beyond the intrinsic—when it teaches us something we didn't know.

As I was writing these pages, I read a *New York Times* obituary of a man named Ira Brilliant, a Brooklyn native who in his life had done many great things, among which was to gather the finest private collection of Beethoven artifacts. I identified strongly with him when he was quoted as describing his feelings upon first seeing Beethoven's signature: "It's one of the most beautiful signatures I've ever seen. . . . The signature sparkled up at me. I washed my fingers and then I touched the letter in the corner and said to myself, 'I have accomplished what I wanted to do.'"

I have experienced that same joy. But I identified even

more strongly with Ira Brilliant when I read that he had acquired a lock of Beethoven's hair, which had both intrinsic value to him as a Beethoven lover and added value when he was able to test the hair and discover high levels of lead. This discovery led some medical historians to conclude that Beethoven may have met his early death—at age fifty-six—from lead poisoning. Not quite the Salieri-Mozart scenario of one musician being murdered by his jealous competitor, because lead was omnipresent in Beethoven's time, but still an addition to history. So the perfect historical find is one that allows the collector not only to hold something touched by, or written by, one of his heroes, but actually to use current expertise to expand our knowledge of the historical figure. I aspired to such a find.

As I was editing this book, I read the posthumously published autobiography of my law school classmate and friend James O. Freedman, the former president of Dartmouth. He, too, was a collector and posed the following question:

> Why is it . . . that some people are collectors—indeed some people seem to have a genetic predisposition to collect—and others are not? Even young children, after all, feel the impulse to collect—baseball cards or postcards, seashells or colored stones, campaign buttons or license plates. And why is it that of those who are collectors, some choose to collect books rather than other objects?[1]

Jim was an eclectic collector who "sometimes . . . wished that [my] collecting habits were less eclectic, so that my collection could achieve a greater coherence or a more specialized focus. But I assured myself that, for now, I was laying the foundations; I could begin to specialize in a later year."

Jim quoted Congressman Cyrus King of Massachusetts during the debate over whether Congress should pay to acquire the great library of Thomas Jefferson: "The bill," he said, "would put $23,900 into Jefferson's pocket for about 6,000 books, good, bad, and indifferent, old, new, and worthless, in languages which many cannot read, and most ought not."[2]

Eventually, my friend Jim concentrated on books, especially autographed ones:

> As my book collection grew—probably to several hundred volumes by the time I entered law school—I came to appreciate the special satisfaction of owning books signed by their authors. John Updike has written of the "fetish of the signature," and decried the burden of facing lines of collectors, clutching one of his books and awaiting his signature, "As if a book, like a check, needs to be signed to be valid."[3]

I, too, loved signed books, letters, and photographs, but I collect almost anything connected to my interests and those of my family. Recently I acquired an actual photograph of the first moment of manned flight, with Orville Wright at the controls and Wilber Wright observing. The photo was taken with Orville Wright's camera and signed by him. My nephew Adam, who is an aeronautical engineer and pilot, will eventually own this important piece of history.

I roam flea markets, used-book stores, garage sales—and now, occasionally, eBay—in search of the perfect purchase. Mostly, I have found memorabilia from my youth—a Captain Midnight Ovaltine mug; a Captain Marvel tie pin; a *Hogan's Heroes* lunch box; a Howdy Doody swimming tube; a Perry Mason cigarette lighter; items from the 1939

This photo with Orville Wright at the controls and Wilbur observing shows the first moment of manned flight. The photo was taken with Wilbur's camera and was signed by Orville.

World's Fair in New York, to which my parents took me in my baby carriage; and assorted comic books (some of which I could swear were the originals thrown out by my mother). When I come upon a piece of nostalgia, it makes my day. I reminisce, I call my old friends to brag about my find, I feel young. Then I feel old, but a good old. I once came across a copy of one of my own books, autographed by me to a friend, who obviously valued it so much that he sold it to a used-book store for two dollars. That didn't make me feel so good.

I thought I had made the perfect buy about five years ago at the Chilmark flea market on Martha's Vineyard, when I found a baseball bat autographed by the 1955 Brooklyn Dodgers—the only Brooklyn Dodgers team to win a World Series. Although the autographs were machine imprinted, still it was an authentic 1955 bat. I bought it from a Protestant minister who earns extra money selling sports memorabilia at flea markets. We discuss the Bible, baseball, and the beach interchangeably. My kind of guy. A man who wanted me to take a case once gave me a Hank Greenberg bat. I took the case. Another guy gave me some Brooklyn Dodgers autographs to encourage me to speak to his group. A school at which I spoke presented me with a framed piece of Ebbets Field. I have several signed baseballs and basketballs

Here I am showing off one of the treasures I found at the Chilmark Flea Market: a 1955 Brooklyn Dodgers autographed bat that I bought from a Protestant minister. The baseball was autographed by Boston Red Sox players.

as well. I also have two old seats from Boston Garden signed by two of my basketball heroes, Larry Bird and Bill Russell. (My grandson Lyle, who is following in my dusty footsteps, talked Barry Bonds into signing his baseball.) This generally has been the nature of my finds and acquisitions.

Then about two years ago, I came upon a real treasure in the New York City flea market on Sixth Avenue and Twenty-fifth Street. A Russian man, from whom I had previously bought some Soviet war medals, called me over and asked, "Do you ever hear about some American president named 'Link-lon?'" (as he pronounced it).

"Sure," I replied, "Abraham Lincoln."

"Well, whatever his name is, do you want to buy a small picture of him?"

Flea markets often have amazing treasures for those willing to look. I found this 1864 Abraham Lincoln campaign medallion at the flea market on Sixth Avenue and Twenty-fifth Street in New York City. The photo of Lincoln is pristine.

I asked to see it, and he produced from his pocket an 1864 campaign medallion, with a photograph of Lincoln on one side (I think it may be by the famous Civil War photographer Mathew Brady) and a photograph of Andrew Johnson, his running mate, on the reverse side. The Johnson photo is a bit damaged, but the Lincoln is pristine. I bargained him down from $400 to $225 and bought it. (I would have paid much more if I'd had to.) It is a remarkable historical item, and up until then my perfect purchase. (It's also my wife's perfect purchase, since it is so tiny.)

Having achieved the nirvana of flea-market purchases— short of an early version of the Declaration of Independence— I thought I was about ready to retire, perhaps not undefeated, since I had bought some fakes and other disappointing objects over the years (particularly on eBay, which provides little

I search for hidden treasures at the Chilmark Flea Market in July 2007.

protection against fraud), but still a tchotchke champion. I quickly discovered, however, that the pull was too strong. I was really addicted. There was something out there—in someone's garage, in an obscure flea market, in an old bookstore— that had my name on it, that I must have.

I continued to patronize the Chilmark flea market when I was on Martha's Vineyard, the Sixth and Ninth Avenue flea markets when I was in New York City, and my favorite used book stores. My passion remained unsated. There was still that one Holy Grail, that impossible flea-market dream, that remnant of a Dead Sea Scroll, that lost item of Americana, that missing piece of some puzzle. I had to find it.

And I did. On September 8, 2006, in an old bookstore in New York.

This is the story of what I found, how I found it, and why it is so important to me—and to history. But first, a few words about my other passion in life—my professional passion as a lawyer and a teacher—and how my two passions were simultaneously satisfied by what I found in that New York bookstore on that hot September day.

2

My Passions for Freedom of Speech, Criminal Law, and Thomas Jefferson

I became a law teacher at the age of twenty-five. Some of my students were older than I was. (My early students included William Bennett, David Gergen, Liddy Dole, Elizabeth Holtzman, Jane Harmon, John Sexton, and Joel Klein. More recent students included Eliot Spitzer, Russell Feingold, and Jeffrey Toobin.) Harvard hired me right out of a Supreme Court clerkship and without any practical experience as a lawyer. I accepted the offer because I was scared that Harvard would change its mind after realizing that I didn't know very much about the law, especially about how it was practiced. But Harvard had decided to take a chance with me because of the three *Law Journal* articles I had written as a Yale Law School student.

Those articles had a common theme, and the Harvard faculty saw in this thread the potential for a different way of looking at the criminal law. The traditional approach of the criminal law was *reactive*—to wait until a crime was committed and then to apprehend the criminal and punish that person for his or her past crime in order to *deter* others (and the criminal) from committing future crimes. The punishment, if it was imprisonment or execution, would also *incapacitate* the criminal (at least, during his or her term of imprisonment), thus preventing this individual from committing future crimes (at least, against people outside of prison). There were, of course, certain criminal laws that were somewhat more *proactive* or *preventive*, such as the laws of attempt, conspiracy, incitement, and solicitation. These laws sought to nip crimes in the bud, by punishing dangerous conduct before it blossomed into full-grown harm, such as murder or rape.

Early in my career, while perusing a first edition of Lewis Carroll's *Alice in Wonderland*, I came across the following argument that Carroll had the Queen make to Alice:

> "[T]here's the King's Messenger. He's in prison now, being punished; and the trial doesn't begin till next Wednesday; and of course the crime comes last of all."
>
> "Suppose he never commits the crime?" said Alice.
>
> "That would be all the better, wouldn't it?" the Queen said. . . .
>
> Alice felt there was no denying that. "Of course that would be all the better," she said. "But it wouldn't be all the better his being punished."

"You're wrong . . . ," said the Queen. "Were *you* ever punished?"

"Only for faults," said Alice.

"And you were all the better for it, I know!" the Queen said triumphantly.

"Yes, but then I *had* done the things I was punished for," said Alice: "that makes all the difference."

"But if you *hadn't* done them," the Queen said, "that would have been even better still; better, and better, and better!" Her voice went higher with each "better," till it got quite to a squeak. . . .

Alice [thought]. "There's a mistake here somewhere—"[1]

I spent years, and wrote much, trying to figure out what that mistake was and how to correct it.

I became interested particularly in "inchoate," or incomplete, crimes, such as attempts and conspiracies, and I wrote about them for the *Yale Law Journal.* My first note—a short student-written commentary on a recent case—dealt with the law of attempted murder. It was titled "Why Do Criminal Attempts Fail? A New Defense." It was quite sophomoric, but that was okay because I wrote it as a freshman.

The thrust of the article was where to draw the appropriate line between *preparation* to commit a crime, such as murder, and the crime itself. What was the "overt act" required to cross the line between innocence and guilt? Could words alone—threats, incitements, epithets—constitute the required overt act? Or was a physical act, even a harm, necessary?

These are important questions, especially in a society that places so much value on freedom of speech. After all, our

Constitution prohibits the government from making any law abridging the freedom of speech. Yet common sense and experience show that speech can be quite dangerous. We were told as kids that "sticks and stones can break your bones, but names can never harm you." But, of course, names can harm you. The reason we were told they couldn't was to get us to hold in check our instinctive desire to respond to nasty names such as "nigger," "kike," "wop," and so on, with sticks, stones, and fists. In fact, my father taught me to use my fists if anyone called me a kike (or if anyone referred to a "negro" as a "nigger"). The Holocaust and the lynchings in the American South taught us that what begins with dehumanizing words could end with dehumanizing and deadly acts. Speech is not altogether "free." It can have serious consequences. Just ask Alexander Hamilton, who was killed in a duel over words.

But suppression of speech also had consequences. I came of age during the McCarthy period. Some of my teachers were fired for what they believed in or said—or for what they refused to say when they were told to take loyalty oaths or to testify against friends. I understood both sides of the speech conundrum. I had experienced dangerous speech, and I had experienced dangerous censorship. I knew that lines had to be drawn. And I also knew that it would be impossible to draw perfect lines that criminalized only dangerous ("bad") speech without also censoring positive ("good") speech. I was never an *absolute* absolutist on freedom of speech, but I was a *presumptive* absolutist. (Or, to invoke an oxymoron but one that makes a point, I was a "relative absolutist.") All speech should be presumed to be protected by the Constitution, and a heavy burden should be placed on those who would censor to demonstrate with relative certainty that the speech at issue, if not censored, would lead to irremediable and immediate serious harm. No one should be allowed—in the famous but often misused words of Justice Oliver Wendell Holmes Jr.—falsely to shout fire in a crowded theater, but anyone should be allowed to hand out leaflets in front of the theater urging people not to enter because of potential fire hazards.

In 1989, I wrote an article in the *Atlantic Monthly* titled "Shouting Fire," which was highly critical of how the Holmes metaphor has been misapplied over the years, including by Holmes himself in the very case in which he introduced the phrase:

> The example of shouting "Fire!" obviously bore little relationship to the facts in the Schenck case [where the metaphor originated]. The Schenck pamphlet contained a substantive political message. It urged draftee readers to *think* about the message and then—if they so chose—to act on it in a lawful and nonviolent way. The man who shouts "Fire!" in a crowded theater is neither sending a political message nor inviting his listener to think about what he has said and decide what to do in a rational, calculated manner. On the contrary, the message is designed to force action *without* contemplation. The message "Fire!" is directed not to the mind and the conscience of the listener but rather to his adrenaline and his feet. . . . It is—as Justice Holmes recognized in his follow-up sentence—the functional equivalent of "uttering words that have all the effect of force." . . . Indeed, in that respect the shout of "Fire!" is not even speech, in any meaningful sense of that term. . . . Another important reason the analogy is inapt is that Holmes emphasizes the factual falsity of the shout "Fire!" The Schenck pamphlet, however, was

not factually false. It contained political opinions and ideas about the causes of war and about appropriate and lawful responses to the draft. As the Supreme Court reaffirmed in *Falwell v. Hustler*, "the First Amendment recognizes no such thing as a false idea." Nor does it recognize false opinions about the causes of or cures for war.[2]

Early in my career I had been elected to the national board of directors of the American Civil Liberties Union (ACLU), where I struggled with difficult cases that sought to strike the delicate balance between constitutionally protected freedom of speech and unprotected incitement to violence. It was during the Vietnam War and the Nixon scandals, and I almost always struck the balance in favor of speech. The notorious Skokie case of 1977 was the most prominent of the ACLU controversies, and, as a Jew, I caught a lot of flak for defending the rights of neo-Nazis to march through a Jewish neighborhood that was home to many Holocaust survivors. The Nazis had deliberately selected that neighborhood to provoke a highly public controversy—and they succeeded. I took the view that I was defending free speech and opposing censorship—not defending Nazis. My mother didn't buy it.

"Whose side are you on?" she demanded. "The Nazis' or the Jews'?" She was always the best cross-examiner in the family.

My practice as well has focused on drawing the line between free speech and dangerous conduct. My first argument in the Supreme Court, when I was thirty years old, involved the criminal prosecution of individuals responsible for the importation, distribution, and showing of a Swedish anti-war film called *I Am Curious (Yellow)*. It was about a young woman's political and sexual coming of age in the context of her opposition to the Vietnam War. By today's standards, its occasional nudity and sexuality would probably earn it an R rating, but it was regarded as obscene in the 1960s. The argument centered on the distinction between speech and action. A memorable exchange between Chief Justice Warren Burger and me involved "bear-baiting," an activity about which I knew very little.

The chief justice tried to draw an analogy between a physical act—namely, a live bear-baiting contest in which an animal is abused—and a film of a couple engaged in consensual sex. I resisted the analogy and argued that there is an enormous difference between protected speech (the film at issue) and unprotected acts (baiting a bear). But the chief justice persisted with his silly example. The court eventually decided the case on procedural grounds, without reaching a decision based on the speech/act distinction. (A full account appears in my book *The Best Defense*, on pages 165–168.)

In recent years, the important issue of when to draw the line between speech and action has arisen in the context of terrorism. Experience has shown that suicide bombers have often been inspired, if not incited, to violence by radical imams who preach death to infidels and teach that the Koran and the Sharia justify, if not demand, that Muslims be willing to become "shahids"—that is, martyrs—who use their bodies as human bombs. Terrorism also requires long-term planning, and terrorist groups are difficult to infiltrate. The critical questions, therefore, are: At what point can preaching, teaching, or planning terrorism be made a crime? When should the law authorize preemptive or preventive intervention? What is the "overt act" that turns protected speech into punishable crime? Former Speaker of the House Newt Gingrich recently opined that we may have to modify our views of free speech in order to combat terrorism, remarking that the American people needed to have "a serious debate about the First Amendment."[3] Many Americans seem to agree. In a 2006 poll conducted by the First Amendment Center at Vanderbilt University, 40 percent of Americans who were polled agreed that "the press in America has too much freedom to do what it wants." In the same survey, 18 percent "strongly" or "mildly" agreed that "the First Amendment goes too far in the rights it guarantees."

In Great Britain, several controversial proposals have been put forward that would prevent radical imams from preaching violence. Parliament initially enacted the Racial and Religious Hatred Act of 2005, which made a crime of "stirring up hatred against persons on religious grounds," as well as the publishing, distributing, depicting, or broadcasting of any material pursuant to that end. After a persistent outcry from civil libertarian groups, Parliament amended and passed the bill as the Racial and Religious Hatred Act of 2006. This version was softer, having added the *intent* to stir up hatred as a prerequisite, as well as including what Salman Rushdie called a "First Amendment of [Britain's] own"—a provision that explicitly protects Britons' right to self-expression. Oddly, this was called a defeat for Tony Blair and the Labour Party.[4]

I have been personally involved in several cases concerning religious leaders who inspired or incited violence on the part of their followers. The first, back in the 1970s, involved a charismatic right-wing rabbi named Meir Kahane who preached violence against those who, in his view, practiced violence or repression against the Jews of the Soviet Union and of Israel. In several instances, Kahane's followers engaged in violence resulting in at least one death and numerous injuries. I represented one of his followers who was accused of making a smoke bomb that was planted in the office of the music impresario Sol Hurok and that killed one of his employees.[5] It turned out that my client—initially unbeknownst to me or his fellow members of the Jewish Defense League—was a government informer who was playing both sides. We won the case on constitutional grounds, and everyone went free because of government misconduct, but I fundamentally disapproved of what Rabbi Kahane was preaching and understood the government's desire to prosecute him as well as his followers.

More recently, I was asked to represent the leader of the World Church of the Creator, who was denied admission to the Illinois bar because of his neo-Nazi views. Although I found the young man and his views repellent, I was troubled by the power of bar association "character committees" to keep people from becoming lawyers because of their political views. I seriously considered taking the case, but before doing so, I asked the man to agree to a number of preconditions, including these: that I could publicly criticize him and his group at any time without limitation; that if, at any time, I learned that he or his group was involved in any violent activities or advocated violence, I could immediately drop his case; that there would be no confidentiality agreement between us; that my fee would be my standard rate; that any money paid to me for my services would be donated to groups that actively combat his views and those of his organization; and finally, that in representing him, I could associate myself with any counsel of my choice, regardless of race, ethnicity, or sexual orientation. He refused some of these conditions, so we ultimately failed to enter into an agreement, and I did not take the case. He eventually lost his appeal. When he learned of his loss, he met with one of his followers. What he said to this person is not known, but the follower immediately went out and shot nine black, Asian, and Jewish people, two of whom died. The leader was never charged in connection with those racist killings but was eventually convicted of soliciting the murder of a federal judge and sentenced to forty years in prison. Several years later, the FBI warned me that this same leader may have inspired some of his followers to "get" me, and I was guarded by armed FBI agents for several days. This certainly brought home to me how dangerous words could be and how easily they could lead to violence.

Another personal experience also convinced me of the serious dangers of religiously inspired violence. In the fall of 1995, I received a visit from the Israeli ambassador to the United States advising me that the prime minister of Israel, Yitzhak Rabin, was scheduled to speak in Boston the following week and had requested a meeting with me. I asked what it concerned, and the ambassador informed me that Rabin was worried about the escalating rhetoric in Israel. Some extremist rabbis were declaring him to be a *rodef*—a status in Jewish religious law that allegedly authorizes citizens to take justice into their own hands and kill the *rodef* because he was a threat to the Jewish people. Rabin was advocating peace with the Palestinians and a gradual end to the occupation. This was considered treason and heresy by some extremists who believed that God gave the entire land of Israel to the Jewish people. Rabin wanted my advice on whether anything could be done, consistent with principles of free speech, to reduce the escalating rhetoric. He was concerned that it could incite violence. Our meeting to discuss this difficult subject was scheduled for Tuesday, November 14. On November 4, Rabin was murdered by a Jewish law student who had been incited to action by the rabbis and others about whom Rabin was concerned. (I could never bring myself to cross out of my appointment book the scheduled meeting with Rabin.) One rabbi, who placed a curse on Rabin, was charged in connection with Rabin's murder. He was sentenced to four months in prison and a year's suspended sentence for incitement to violence under Israel's Prevention of Terrorism Act.[6]

I have written extensively about those issues. Several of my recent books deal precisely with how to strike the appropriate balance and where to draw the appropriate line between the maximalist civil liberties position, especially with regard to freedom of speech, and the maximalist security position, especially with regard to terrorism. As I wrote in my book *Why Terrorism Works*:

> It is important in this time of danger that those who are in charge of our safety and those who see their role as defending our liberty work together as much as possible to avoid unnecessary conflict. . . . The balances we ultimately strike will contain trade-offs between our liberties and our safety that will not satisfy absolutists in either the law enforcement or the civil libertarian camps. But if we work together—if civil libertarians are brought into the tent in advance, rather than playing their traditional role of criticizing from outside afterward—the beneficiaries will be all Americans who rightly demand both safety and freedom.[7]

In my classes as well, much of the discussion focuses on whether "mere" speech can ever be made a crime, or whether we must wait for an "overt act," and if so, what sort of overt act. I care deeply about freedom of speech, but I am also a realist about terrorism and the threat it poses. I worry that among the first victims of another mass terrorist attack will be civil liberties, including freedom of speech.[8] The right of every citizen to express dissident and controversial views remains a powerful passion in my life. I not only believe in it, I practice it.

Another of my passions—unrelated, I thought, until now—was the belief systems of Thomas Jefferson and his generation of American founders, many of whom were deists who believed in reason more than in faith. I wrote a book called *America Declares Independence*, which deals with the religious and political beliefs of those individuals—especially Jefferson, John Adams, and Benjamin Franklin—who played the most important roles in framing our Declaration of Independence. I am a loyal reader of the wonderful works of my fellow Martha's Vineyarder David McCullough, whose books about the Adamses and George Washington brought me so much reading pleasure (along with his earlier books about my hometown bridge in Brooklyn and one of my favorite presidents, Harry Truman).

I read everything about Jefferson I could get my hands on. He truly was a remarkable man and in many ways the inventor, as distinguished from the discoverer, of the United States. Let me explain the difference between discovery and invention by quoting an argument between Jerry Seinfeld and George Costanza—two of my favorite philosophers—about their favorite explorer:

GEORGE: Magellan? You like Magellan?

JERRY: Oh, yeah. My favorite explorer. Around the world. Come on. Who do you like?

GEORGE: I like de Soto.

JERRY: De Soto? What did he do?

GEORGE: Discovered the Mississippi.

JERRY: Oh, like they wouldn't have found that anyway.

Discovery connotes an existing entity waiting to be found, if only we look in the right place. The physical rules of nature actually exist and await discovery by human beings. (They would, of course, exist even in the absence of human beings, as they did for billions of years. They just would not be called "rules" because there would be no one to understand or even name them.) Isaac Newton discovered some, Albert Einstein others, and Charles Darwin yet others. If these giants had not discovered these rules when they did, it is reasonable to assume that other geniuses would have made these (or similar) discoveries since the rules of nature are out there waiting to be discovered, just as some European would have found the Mississippi River even if Hernando de Soto had somehow missed it. Seinfeld, it turns out, was right.

Inventions are different. They require the creative combining of different kinds of knowledge and information—both theoretical and practical—to design something that did not previously exist. Simple inventions, such as the cotton gin or the internal combustion engine, would have been made by others, if the people responsible for inventing them had never lived. Complex, more individualistic inventions, such as Beethoven's symphonies, Picasso's paintings, and Shakespeare's plays, would never have been replicated by others, at least not exactly. They are truly unique. We call them "inspired," but they are human inventions. There are also, of course, many things that fall somewhere between discovery and invention. Columbus (or Eriksson) discovered America. If they hadn't, someone else would have. Jefferson (along with James Madison, Alexander Hamilton, and others) invented the America we now know.

I will always remember President John F. Kennedy's famous greeting to a group of brilliant intellectuals whom he invited to the White House dining room, in which he described them as the greatest assemblage of intellects ever to gather in the White House since Jefferson dined there alone. (That, in contrast to John Maynard Keynes's statement about David Lloyd George: "When he's alone in a room, there's nobody there," or what Winston Churchill said about the man who defeated him for office: "An empty taxi arrived at 10 Downing Street, and when the door opened Clement Attlee got out.")[9]

I have also written about the conflict that emerged between Jefferson and Adams over the Sedition Acts of 1798, which punished a wide array of allegedly seditious speech without waiting for any overt act to occur. Adams supported the law and sought to enforce it vigorously against his political enemies. Jefferson opposed the law and refused to apply it when he became president.[10] His decision to pardon all those who had been convicted under what he regarded as an unconstitutional law led to a sharp exchange between the new president and the wife of his predecessor, as I will show in the next chapter.

I have also written about recent efforts by the religious right to hijack the Declaration of Independence. Its members are desperately seeking to re-create in their own images the founding fathers who wrote the Declaration, in an effort to misinform the public into believing that the United States was established as a Christian nation based on the Bible.[11] These revisionists are trying to convert our charter of liberty into a baptismal certificate. In order to do so, they must distort, rewrite, oversimplify, and sometimes fabricate the rich history of our Declaration. Jefferson is the key to understanding the new republic that our founding fathers sought to invent. Just days before his death on the fiftieth anniversary of the Declaration of Independence, Jefferson explained what he believed was the essence of the transforming document and what he hoped it would mean to future generations:

> May it be to the world, what I believe it will be, (to some parts sooner, to others later, but finally to all,) the signal of arousing men to burst the chains under which monkish ignorance and superstition had persuaded them to bind themselves, and to assume the blessings and security of self-government. That form which we have substituted, restores the free right to the unbounded exercise of reason and freedom of opinion. All eyes are opened, or opening, to the rights of man. The general spread of the light of science has already laid open to every view the palpable truth, that the mass of mankind has not been born with saddles on their backs, nor a favored few booted and spurred, ready to ride them legitimately, by the grace of God. These are grounds of hope for others. For ourselves, let the annual return of this day forever refresh our recollections of these rights, and an undiminished devotion to them.[12]

It is hard to reconcile this ringing endorsement of "reason" over "superstition" and this condemnation of "monkish ignorance" with an America as a biblical theocracy. Jefferson and his generation of founders hoped that future generations of Americans would continue to arouse men and women to "burst the chains" of "ignorance and superstition" and to live lives of "reason and freedom," guided by "the light of science." These are, of course, generalities, and over the last few years, I have asked myself what Jefferson might say, if he were alive today, about a diverse array of specific contemporary issues.[13] Most particularly, how would he respond if asked for guidance on how to strike the proper balance, where to draw the appropriate line, between dangerous speech and harmful conduct, especially in the context of incitements to terrorism? I was not aware of anything he had written that would provide clear guidance as to how he may have thought about these issues. I have also written about the risks of speculating with regard to how a long-dead historical figure might see current issues in the very different context of the world in which we now live, but I cannot help wondering, to paraphrase a current religious mantra, what would Jefferson have done?

Imagine my surprise, and joy, when my passions merged on that September day and I found, in the old bookstore, an original and unpublished letter by Thomas Jefferson dealing precisely with the issue of where to draw the line between advocacy and action, between preaching and practice, between speech and "overt act." It was almost as if Jefferson, who has always been among my heroes (his picture has long hung next to Jackie Robinson's in my office), had written the letter to me, in response to my persistent questions.

Let me now tell you how I came upon this letter and exactly what it says.

PART
II

THE LETTER

3

——⟫●⟪——

Finding the
Jefferson Letter

The Argosy Bookstore—"A 6 story 19th century structure with a funny indented arcade"[1]—is a New York City landmark that has been in the Cohen family for generations. It has been "designated one of the top 10 reasons to remain in New York. And yet, were one to stop, say, a hundred randomly chosen East Siders and ask, 'What's your favorite bookstore?' or 'Which are the best bookstores in the city?' few would name Argosy."[2]

It is, apparently, one of New York's best-kept secrets. Located in a stately building on East Fifty-ninth Street, it describes itself as a purveyor of "old and rare books," and it is certainly that. As Michael Thomas, one Argosy admirer, wrote, if his library burned down—as Jefferson's did when he was a young man[3]—he would know where to go to replace it:

> Even before the insurance check arrived, I would be heading straight to East 59th Street, where, under a banner first flown (metaphorically at least) fourscore years ago, the Argosy Book Shop performs its biblio-philic magic. There, I would genuflect before the three stunning sisters—Judith Lowery, Naomi Hample, and Adina Cohen—who own and operate Argosy, founded by and inherited from their father, Louis, whose man-tle as a bookselling legend they wear with spirit and elegance, and I would say to them, "My ladies, I need a library."
>
> I would tell them what my interests were, how I want my shelves to look, my likes and dislikes visually and literarily—and then, if I chose, I'd go off on a cruise, secure in the expectation that on my return Judith, Naomi, and Adina would (like another three sisters in literature who come to mind) have conjured me up a proper library, one with range and variety, with many volumes as interesting for themselves as for the words they contain.[4]

In fact, Bill Clinton did just that when a pipe burst in his Chappaqua home, flooding his library:

> "Many of these books were waterlogged, totally ruined," explains Adina Cohen, the youngest of the three sisters who own the store. But as shopkeepers and citizens alike know all too well, what Bill Clinton wants, Bill Clinton gets. Cohen and her staff set out

on a year-long project to replace or repair every one of the damaged titles. Sometimes this meant combing estate sales and calling book dealers for the exact same edition and format of the books the president had lost; sometimes it meant laying hundreds of books literally out to dry.[5]

Argosy's history as a bookstore traces its roots back to 1927, when Louis opened his first place of business along "bookstore row" on Fourth Avenue, where I used to browse as a high school and college student. He moved uptown several years later. In the 1950s, he bought the building on Fifty-ninth Street. Over Argosy's long and distinguished history, its customers have included Franklin Delano Roosevelt, Jacqueline Kennedy, Bill Clinton, Edmund Wilson, Saul Bellow, Katharine Hepburn, Paul Newman, Stephen Sondheim, and even Michael Jackson (who, not surprisingly, collects books about Peter Pan). It's an old-fashioned book store that bears little resemblance to current megachains. It smells like an old library. One of the sisters put it this way: "Isn't the smell of old books wonderful? . . . People say it's musty, but that's not it at all. It's a smell made up of glue and old paper, of course, but also a sense of interiors of life going on inside things, between covers. It's a smell you can just drink in."[6]

Another sister had a different slant: "We don't really run a secondhand bookstore. It's more something else. I'm not entirely sure what. A kind of library, maybe, with the books for sale."

One manifestation of the Argosy's quaintness is in its categories. All books that have anything to do with sex are still classified under "Curiosa." The "library" has more than 200,000 books for sale, ranging from first editions that could set you back several hundred thousand dollars to free books in a barrel. Over the years, I have bought many books as gifts for friends, on subjects ranging from fishing to Groucho Marx. But Argosy is more than a bookstore; it is also a print shop, which is located on the second floor. A recent newspaper account described it:

> On this floor, the myriad list of print subjects has grown to include accounting, barrels, barbers, bridges, bullfighting, canals, candles, windmills, disasters, hydraulics, cotton, birds by type, and birds by artists. The walls are decorated with colorful prints such as one with a man balancing a chair on his chin, long tables— the kind found in reading rooms of libraries—all room for perusing the voluminous selections.[7]

On a recent visit to the print department, the woman in charge showed me a collection of Persian prints with Hebrew writing and inquired whether I knew what they were. I asked where Argosy had gotten them from, but she had no idea. "They've been here for decades. No one knows where they came from." I translated some of the Hebrew— it was from the Bible—and speculated that the prints might be from a children's book that was used in a nineteenth-century Persian Hebrew school.

Finally, Argosy boasts a fine collection of autographs and documents. Good customers are shown—by appointment only—to a rickety old elevator that can hold four people who recently completed Weight Watchers, or three average-sized customers. After a slow ascent to the sixth floor, the door opens to a treasure trove of framed autographs, photographs, and the rarest of documents. It's like visiting a museum or an archive. The collection is extraordinarily eclectic, ranging from a photograph of Picasso (on a postcard) with a beard and a mustache drawn in ballpoint pen by Picasso himself and signed by him, to a check for $50,000 made out to, and endorsed by, Franklin Delano Roosevelt. (Naomi Hample asked me whether I could figure out why anyone would send a check for $50,000 to a sitting president; I'm still working on that one.) There are autographed pictures of ballplayers (Babe Ruth, Ted Williams, Lou Gehrig), magicians (Houdini, Thurston), scientists (Edison, Marconi, Salk), actors (Orson Welles, Laurence Olivier, Sarah Bernhardt), presidents (Washington, Madison, Lincoln, Taft, Ford, Clinton), kings and queens (George, Mary, Elizabeth), prime ministers (Ben-Gurion, Churchill), Supreme Court justices (Black, Douglas, Jackson, Goldberg, Frankfurter, Brandeis), astronauts (Glenn, Grissom), and notorious criminals such as Dillinger, Bonnie and Clyde, and Meyer Lansky. (Some categories, such as those that include Richard Nixon and Spiro Agnew, overlap.) As one customer quipped to Naomi, "Do you know the DNA that's in this room?"

The real treasures, however, are not on the walls but in the locked drawers and files to which only the three sisters have access. Some of these treasures—letters and documents—have been in the family for so many years that Naomi has difficulty locating them. (I think she uses my filing system—I know where it is when I find it.) It took her half an hour to find the FDR check, but I never mind waiting in a room with so many fascinating photographs and autographs.

Over the years, I have bought a photograph signed by David Ben-Gurion (in Hebrew), a letter from Louis Brandeis, and signed photos of several baseball players. I have bought an eighteenth-century prescription for a doctor-friend, an autographed photo of Clarence Darrow for a lawyer, a signed picture of Dr. Jonas Salk for my doctor, and a signed copy of an old Academy Awards program for my son, the film producer. I rarely leave the store empty-handed, but until that September day, I had never made what I consider a major purchase from Naomi and her sisters.

My son, Elon, and I had just finished lunch in a midtown restaurant with a mutual friend, and I was supposed to return uptown to meet my wife at Sotheby's, where impressionist art was on display for an upcoming auction. But Carolyn called to tell me that she had seen nothing interesting, and it would probably not be worth my while to come uptown. So I asked my son whether he would mind a brief stop at Argosy, which was a block away, before we walked home. He agreed, but then my cell phone rang and, for a moment, I forgot about Argosy and started walking toward my apartment. Elon asked me whether I had changed my mind about Argosy, and I said no, I had just forgotten. It certainly wasn't a Freudian slip. Indeed, it shows how close I came to missing the greatest acquisition of my career as a collector. So off we went to Argosy, and Naomi was there. I asked my perennial question: "Got anything I might be interested in?"

She told me about the Roosevelt check and asked me whether I would take a look at it. I told her I wasn't interested in buying it, but I would try to help her figure out what it could be.

I then asked whether she had anything related to the Brooklyn Dodgers, Israel, the Supreme Court, the Declaration of Independence, or Thomas Jefferson. I told her that I had written a book about the Declaration and was in the process of writing another about the misuses of the Declaration by the religious right.

Naomi's face lit up. "Jefferson! I just got a Jefferson letter about freedom of religion. In fact, as soon as I saw it, I thought of you. I would love for you to own it. It was written for you."

I said, "That's great. I'm writing about Jefferson's views on religion. Does it say anything interesting?"

"I think so," she replied. "But you would know better than me. Why don't you read it and tell me."

She opened a locked drawer and produced a file containing a plastic-covered brown-colored paper, worn with age. But clear as day was the well-known signature of "Th Jefferson." It was written on July 3, 1801—the eve of the twenty-fifth anniversary of the Declaration of Independence. She gave me a handwritten copy of the letter to read. I took it in my hand and read it slowly, savoring every word. It was written to Mr. Elijah Boardman. The name was familiar, but I couldn't place it. I later learned that Boardman (1760–1823) was a prominent Connecticut political figure who eventually served as United States senator from Connecticut between 1821 and 1823. At the time that he received the letter, Boardman was "engaged in mercantile pursuits" and would soon be elected to the state House of Representatives. A large painting of this patriot, who, as a young man, had served in the Revolutionary War, is owned by the Metropolitan Museum of Art.

Boardman had written to the recently elected president on June 18, 1801. Jefferson had been elected by an absolute majority of the House of Representatives on its thirty-sixth ballot on February 17, 1801, after the electoral college vote was tied at 73 votes apiece for Jefferson and Aaron Burr. The tie in the initial electoral vote had been "accidental" because of a flaw in the Constitution, under which each elector voted for two candidates "without indicating which was his choice

*Elijah Boardman, 1789. Portrait by Ralph Earl
(1751–1801). Oil on canvas; 83 × 51 inches
(210.8 × 129.5 cm).*

for President and which for Vice President."[8] The incumbent, John Adams, had been eliminated by coming in third in the electoral college balloting. Jefferson was inaugurated on March 4, 1801.

Boardman enclosed in his letter a printed copy of a sermon delivered by the Reverend Stanley Griswold, the pastor of a church in New Milford, Connecticut. The sermon had been published in 1800 and was titled "Truth Its Own Test and God Its Only Judge, or, An Inquiry,— How Far Men May Claim Authority over Each Other's Religious Opinions?"

Reverend Stanley Griswold (1763–1815) was a popular preacher and a rare religious admirer of Jefferson. Many clerics regarded Jefferson as an atheist (which he was not). During the campaign of 1800, one campaign slogan said the choice was between "Adams and God and Jefferson and no God." Jefferson, in fact, believed in God, but his god was the god of nature rather than of the Bible. In a famous sermon delivered at the time Jefferson assumed the presidency titled "Overcoming Evil with Good," Griswold singled out the new president as an example of how evil could be overcome by good:

> Give me leave on this occasion particularly to point you to Thomas Jefferson as a laudable example of that magnanimous and peaceable conduct which I have recommended to you in this discourse, and which is so peculiarly necessary to be put in practice at the present juncture.—That he has been abused, I suppose will be acknowledged on all hands.—But have you heard of his complaining? Have you heard him talk of vengeance and retaliation?"

I recently purchased an original of this sermon "delivered . . . before a numerous collection of friends of the constitution, of Thomas Jefferson, president, and of Aaron Burr, vice-president of the United States."[9] Griswold himself was subsequently "excluded from the association of ministers of which he was a member on account of his alleged heterodoxy."[10] His congregants, however, continued to support him, and he continued to preach until he resigned in 1802. Soon thereafter, he left the ministry and entered politics, briefly filling a vacancy to serve as United States senator from Ohio between 1809 and 1810.[11]

The sermon to which Jefferson was responding (and which is excerpted in appendix B) covered a wide range of issues dealing with beliefs, opinions, expression, teaching, preaching, action, and crime. In the style of the time, it was as much a political speech as a religious sermon, though its references were largely biblical. In general, Griswold took a position supportive of freedom of belief and expression, but on pages 10 and 11, he drew a distinction between "what is *strictly opinion*" and "the *divulging* of an opinion with a wanton view to excite broils and cause needless dissentions, or to influence others to do evil." (Emphasis added.) In other words, the reverend, while acknowledging that everyone had the right to believe in anything they wanted to, if they expressed certain immoral or dangerous opinions, they could be punished. It is this critical distinction—a distinction that was accepted at the time by those regarded by historians as "traditionalists" but rejected by the "new libertarians"[12]—about which Jefferson wrote in his response to Boardman.

The American historian Leonard Levy has written extensively about this distinction. He has concluded that the "new libertarians"—who in Levy's view included such luminaries as George Hay (whom Jefferson appointed U.S. attorney for Virginia, and who prosecuted Aaron Burr for treason), John Thomson (who wrote An *Enquiry Concerning the Liberty and Licentiousness of the Press and the Uncontrollable Nature of the Human Mind*), Tunis Wortman (a New York City lawyer who wrote a number of tracts defending press freedom), and James Madison—"advocated that only 'injurious conduct,' as manifested by 'overt acts' or deeds, rather than words, might be criminally redressable." The traditionalists, on the other hand, argued that immoral or dangerous words alone, if expressed publicly, could be punishable. Levy believed that Jefferson, unlike the "new libertarians," refused to extend the overt-act test to political speech, limiting it only to religious expression. The Jefferson letter that I found at the Argosy Bookstore suggests that the conventional wisdom regarding Jefferson's views on this matter may well be erroneous.

Before we turn to the Jefferson letter itself, let us see precisely what Griswold said on the pages with which Jefferson disagreed:

> The [free speech] position therefore is doubtless true with respect to what is strictly opinion, that a man ought not to be molested in any shape for his opinions, be they what they may. But, the divulging of an opinion with the wanton view to excite broils and cause needless dissentions, or to influence others to do evil, is quite a different thing. This is an overt act, and, as the case may be, an evident immorality. Yet this, I believe, is often confounding in the question, how far men are liable for their opinions? And tends not a little to embarrass the subject of free toleration.

Having thus distinguished between privately held opinions and publicly divulged ones, Griswold proceeded to argue that only some divulged opinions should be deemed punishable.

> But I beg not to be understood as if the promulging of an opinion with an honest view were blamable and

immoral. A person may be honest in divulging some kinds of opinions, believing them to be highly important to be known and embraced by mankind. In this he is no schismatic; he does not from the wanton desire to embroil society and throw it into divisions and confusion: but is serious and sincere, like the apostles of old. No more than the apostles ought such an one to be molested.

But certain opinions may be attempted to be propagated; in which no honest view can possibly exist, and for which a person would justly be accountable to [illegible]. To know what these are, brings up once more the necessity of a line.

Having determined that a line was needed between *protected* and *punishable* expression of views, Griswold proceeded to describe where the line should be drawn.

What then is the line which should divide those opinions which may be promulgated with impunity, from those which cannot be propagated without guilt?

This line I hold to be very plain, even so plain that "he who runs may read it." I believe there is such a thing as a Conscience in man, an inherent sense of right and wrong in every intelligent creature through the world. Some speculatists have pretended to doubt the reality of such a principal in man; but were never able to divest themselves of it. The scriptures clearly recognize this principal, calling it "the law written on the heart." They speak of "the thoughts of men either accusing or else excusing one another," and of the "Gentiles doing by nature the things contained in the law," and of their "being a law unto themselves."

We all feel this principle operating with a sure and uncontrollable sway within us. It is indeed a Monitor and a Vice-Gerent of God almighty in the soul. I suppose it to be inseparable from rational faculties. When we do good, it approves and speaks peace to the mind. When we do evil, it condemns and torments.

This, then, is the line I would have to divide between opinions, to separate those the teaching of which shall be punishable, from those that may be taught with impunity. On the one side are all those things concerning which conscience dictates something. On the other are all those things concerning which it dictates nothing.

This was the traditionalist position on freedom of conscience and expression, set out clearly by one of its most articulate advocates. Reverend Griswold then offered an example that is highly relevant to today's concerns about imams preaching hatred and justifying terrorism:

If a person should endeavor to propagate an opinion, that it is right to steal, to lie, to cheat, to rob, to murder, or to do anything which conscience, or "the law written on the heart," plainly condemns, such person, when though he himself be not guilty of these crimes in an overt form, yet justly subjects himself to the reprehension and censure of all his fellow creatures, and as the case may be I believe to some severer punishment. Could we be content to have a person of this description run about and inculcate these crimes upon our children and upon simple ones? Certainly we could not and ought not. Such an one ought to be taken up and if he will not cease to teach these things, he should not only be censured and reprimanded, but absolutely confined from running at large to poison society and unhinge it from its formulations. Such an one I believe would be liable upon good principles of law and reason to be punished as an accessory, at least as an adviser and mover of the crimes of his pupil. Suppose one of his simple disciples should commit murder, and it should appear that he did it in consequence of what this person had taught him on that subject; although perhaps it should not be sufficient to hang the teacher, yet it ought to subject him to some kind of punishment, and I think of considerable severity.

These concerns, though perhaps somewhat hypothetical at the beginning of the nineteenth century, became all too real at the beginning of the twenty-first century. (As we shall soon see, they were anything but hypothetical to Jefferson near the end of the eighteenth century.) They certainly were real to me as a result of my involvement in the Kahane, the Church of the Creator, and the Rabin tragedies. In each of these cases, the "simple disciples" of one of the religious leaders "did commit murder" and it does "appear that he did in consequence of what this person had taught him." These cases fit properly into Griswold's paradigm for punishment.

It was on this issue of preaching immorality and violence, and the appropriate consequences to the preacher, that Jefferson wrote his letter to Boardman disagreeing with Reverend Griswold. I now present Jefferson's response to Boardman in full. (Jefferson wrote it in the style of the time, referring to himself in the third person, though in his own hand, as proved by an expert handwriting comparison with other letters known to be handwritten by Jefferson.) It is well known that Jefferson always wrote his own letters, except during certain periods when he was unable to. In 1801, when he replied to Boardman, he handwrote his correspondence. Silvio Bedini, who wrote a book on Jefferson's writing habits, summarized his writing history:

> Throughout his public life he personally wrote all of his communications and made his own summaries, and later copies, of letters sent. During this period he employed a male secretary, but as he explained in 1804 to William A. Burwell, a candidate for the position, "the office itself is more in the nature of an Aid de camp than a mere Secretary. The writing is not considerable, because I write my own letters and copy them in a press. . . ." There were only several limited periods in Jefferson's life during which he made use of secretaries or clerks to prepare letters for him. . . . There were also one or two brief intervals when he was physically unable to write his own letters, such as when he broke his wrist in a fall in 1786 and again in 1822. In the final months of his life another accident made it increasingly difficult for him to write, and it was done for him by Nicholas P. Trist, a grandson-in-law who was his constant companion and secretary during his last two years.[13]

Jefferson began his letter to Boardman by commending Griswold on his general thesis in support of freedom of belief and expression: "Th Jefferson returns his thanks to Mr. Boardman for Mr. Griswold's sermon on religious freedom enclosed in his letter of the 18th of June. he had before received it through another channel, & had read with great satisfaction the demonstrative truths it contains."

Jefferson then expressed his disagreement with the pages quoted previously:

[T]o the 10th and 11th pages however he could not assent; and supposes that the respectable & able author, finding himself supported by the good sense of his countrymen as far as he had gone, will see that he may safely, in this part also, go the whole length of sound principle that he will consequently retract the admission that the utterance of an opinion is an overt act, and, if evidently immoral may be punished by law of which evidence too *conscience* is made the umpire[.] [Emphasis in original.]

Jefferson then offered an observation as to how Griswold's proposal would work in practice:

[H]e will reflect that in practice it is the conscience of the judge, & not of the speaker, which will be the umpire. The conscience of the judge then becomes the standard of morality, & the law is to punish what squares not with that standard. [T]he line is to be drawn by that; it will vary with the varying consciences of the same or of different judges & will totally prostrate the rights of conscience in others.

Jefferson proceeded to explain his position: "But we have nothing to fear from the demoralizing reasonings of some, if others are left free to demonstrate their errors. and especially when the law stands ready to punish the first criminal *act* produced by the false reasoning." (Emphasis in original.)

Jefferson then added the following sentence as an interliniation—perhaps an afterthought: "These are safer correctives than the conscience of a judge."

He ended the letter with his salutation, "[H]e prays Mr. Boardman to accept his salutations and respect."

As soon as I read the Jefferson letter, I knew I was on to

a significant discovery. Not only did the letter make several important points about freedom of speech and conscience, but some of them were not familiar to me (and to historians such as Levy) as being Jefferson's views. I knew that Jefferson had opposed the Sedition Act of 1798, but his public opposition was based largely on his position with regard to *federalism*: he strongly believed that the *federal* government lacked the power to punish seditious speech; the *states*, on the other hand, had broad authority to decide what could be punished. He expressed this far more structural and narrow view of freedom of speech in a feisty exchange of letters with Abigail Adams several years later. (By "structural," I mean his views of the proper structure of our federal government, which he believed allocated most powers, including the power to regulate seditious speech, to the states.)

On July 1, 1804, Abigail Adams wrote to Jefferson, complaining about his decision to pardon a man named James Thomson Callender, a pamphleteer who had been convicted and sentenced to prison for nine months and a fine of $200 for libeling John Adams:

> One of the first acts of your administration was to liberate a wretch who was suffering the just punishment of the Law due to his crimes for writing and publishing the basest libel, the lowest and vilest Slander, which malice could invent, or calumny exhibit against the Character and reputation of your predecessor, of him for whom you profest the highest esteem and Friendship, and whom you certainly knew incapable of such complicated baseness. The remission of Callenders fine was a public approbation of his conduct. Is not the last restraint of vice, a sense of shame, rendered abortive, if abandoned Characters do not excite abhorrence. If the chief Majestrate of a Nation, whose elevated Station

places him in a conspicuous light, and renders his every action a concern of general importance, permits his public conduct to be influenced by private resentment, and so far forgets what is due to his Character as to give countanance to a base Calumniater, is he not answerable for the influence which his example has upon the manners and morals of the community?[14]

On July 22, 1804, Jefferson responded to Abigail Adams's complaint:

that I "liberated a wretch who was suffering for a libel against Mr. Adams." I do not know who was the particular wretch alluded to: but I discharged every person under punishment or prosecution under the Sedition law, because I considered and now consider that law to be a nullity as absolute and as palpable as if Congress had ordered us to fall down and worship a golden image; and that it was as much my duty to arrest it's execution in every stage, as it would have been to have rescued from a fiery furnace those who should have been cast into it for refusing to worship their image. It was accordingly done in every instance, without asking what the offenders had done, or against whom they had offended, but whether the pains they were suffering were inflicted under the pretended Sedition law.

Abigail Adams replied on August 18, 1804, as follows:

Your statement respecting Callender (who was the wretch referred to) and your motives for liberating him, wear a different aspect as explaind by you from the impression which they had made, not only upon my mind, but upon the minds of all those, whom I ever heard speak upon the subject. With regard to the act under which he was punished, different persons entertain different opinions respecting it. It lies not with me to decide upon its validity. That I presume devolved upon the supreme Judges of the Nation: but I have understood that the power which makes a Law, is alone competent to the repeal. If a Chief Majestrate can by his will annul a Law, where is the difference between a republican, and a despotic Government? That some restraint should be laid upon the asassin [*sic*], who stabs reputation, all civilized Nations have assented to. In no Country has calumny falshood and revileing stalked abroad more licentiously, than in this. No political Character has been secure from its attacks no reputation so fair, as not to be wounded by it, untill truth and falshood lie in one undistinguished heap. If there are no checks to be restored to the Laws of the Land, and no reperation to be made to the injured, will not Man become the judge and avenger of his own wrongs, and as in a late instance, the sword and pistol decide the contest? [Referring, no doubt, to the duel between Alexander Hamilton and Aaron Burr, fought on July 11, 1804, in which Hamilton was killed.] All the Christian and social virtues will be banished the Land. All that makes Life desirable, and softens the ferocious passions of Man will assume a savage deportment, and like Cain of old every Mans hand will be against his Neighbour." [Bracketed passage from *The Adams-Jefferson Letters*.][15]

Jefferson wrote back on September 11, 1804:

You seem to think it devolved on the judges to decide on the validity of the sedition law. But nothing in the constitution has given them the right to decide for the executive, more than to the Executive to decide for them. Both magistracies are equally independent in the sphere of action assigned to them. The judges, believing the law constitutional, had a right to pass a sentence of fine and imprisonment, because that power was placed in their hands by the constitution. But the Executive, believing the law to be unconstitutional, was bound to remit the execution of it; because that power has been confided to him by the constitution. That instrument meant that it's co-ordinate branches should be checks on each other. But the opinion which gives to the judges the right to decide what laws are constitutional, and what not, not only for themselves in their own sphere of action, but for the legislature and executive also in their spheres, would make the judiciary a despotic branch.[16]

At the time Jefferson made this argument, it was considered a "liberal" point, because judges were regarded as the most conservative elements in our government. Jefferson's political enemy Chief Justice John Marshall arrogated to the judiciary the ultimate power to decide the constitutionality of laws. Today, Jefferson's argument is deemed quite conservative, having been offered up by opponents of court-imposed integration, choice on abortion, and the separation of church and state. Some, like former U.S. Attorney General Edwin Meese, take Jefferson's stance to the extreme, arguing that "Supreme Court decisions might be binding only on the parties to a case," severely limiting or even eliminating the Court's power to settle general constitutional questions and set precedent.[17]

Jefferson then went on to draw a sharp distinction between the power of the *federal* government to punish defamatory speech and the powers of the *states* to do so:

> Nor does the opinion of the unconstitutionality and consequent nullity of that law remove all restraint from the overwhelming torrent of slander which is confounding all vice and virtue, all truth and falsehood in the US. The power to do that is fully possessed by the several state legislatures. It was reserved to them, and was denied to the general government, by the constitution according to our construction of it. While we deny that Congress have a right to control the freedom of the press, we have ever asserted the right of the states, and their exclusive right, to do so. They have accordingly, all of them, made provisions for punishing slander, which those who have time and inclination resort to for the vindication of their characters.

Jefferson did express his personal opposition to state laws that did not allow truth as a defense: "In general the state laws appear to have made the presses responsible for slander as far as it is consistent with their useful freedom. In those states where they do not admit even the truth of allegations to protect the printer, they have gone too far."

In other words, Jefferson said to Mrs. Adams that he believed the states should punish false defamatory speech but not truthful defamatory speech. The law of the day generally made no such distinction. Indeed, some authorities argued that truthful defamation was more damaging than false defamation. The most famous example of this is in the 1734 trial of John Peter Zenger in New York. Zenger published a weekly newspaper that printed criticisms of the royal governor; although he did not write the offending articles, the governor sued him for "seditious libel" against the king's government. When Zenger's counsel acknowledged that Zenger had in fact printed the material, with the defense that it was all true, the attorney for the Crown responded, "[A]s [Zenger] has confessed the Printing and Publishing these Libels, I think the Jury must find a Verdict for the King; for supposing they were true, the Law says that they are not the less libellous for that; nay indeed the Law says, their being true is an Aggravation of the Crime."[18]

Abigail Adams got the last word on this subject in her letter of October 25, 1804: "I cannot agree, in opinion, that the constitution ever meant to withhold from the National Government the power of self defence, or that it could be considerd an infringement of the Liberty of the press, to punish the licentiousness of it."[19]

Abigail Adams expressed the federalist argument that freedom of speech and of the press could be defined only by the English common law, and that the First Amendment had not deprived Congress of the power to pass a sedition law. The Republicans argued that the First Amendment "not only rejected the English common law concept of libels against the government but also prohibited congress from adding any restraint either by previous restrictions, by subsequent punishment, or by an alteration of jurisdiction or mode of trial."[20]

She continued, "Time Sir must determine, and posterity judge with more candour, and impartiality, I hope than the conflicting parties of our day, what measures have best promoted the happiness of the people what raised them from a state of depression and degradation to wealth, honor, and reputation; what has made them affluent at home, and respected abroad, and to whom ever the tribute is due to them may it be given." (Actually, the last word was had by

John Adams, who appended the following note: "Quincy Nov. 19 1804. The whole of this correspondence was begun and conducted without my knowledge or suspicion. Last evening and this morning at the desire of Mrs. Adams I read the whole. I have no remarks to make upon it at this time and in this place. J. Adams")

Jefferson's acknowledgment of the power of the states to restrict freedom of speech was not merely hypothetical. As a legislator in Virginia during the Revolution, he supported (and possibly wrote) a measure criminalizing speech in support of the British Crown and punishing it by "five years imprisonment and a fine of £20,000"; he also supported a bill that required a loyalty oath from all adult men in Virginia, without which they would be subject to triple taxation and the loss of their political rights.[21] In 1798, during the controversy over the Alien and Sedition Acts—which provided broad power to punish speech critical of the federal government—Jefferson famously argued against the acts (as he later wrote to Abigail Adams), not because they abridged speech, but because the power to regulate speech belonged to the states alone. He did so, anonymously, in writing the Kentucky Resolutions—a companion to James Madison's Virginia Resolutions—against the Alien and Sedition Acts. Jefferson and Madison collaborated on these resolutions and submitted them anonymously to the Kentucky and Virginia legislatures, which then made them law. In the Kentucky Resolution, Jefferson called the acts null and void:

[T]hat no power over the freedom of religion, freedom of speech, or freedom of the press being delegated to the United States by the Constitution, nor prohibited by it to the states, all lawful powers respecting the same did of right remain, and were reserved to the states, or to the people: That thus was manifested their determination to retain to themselves the right of judging how far the licentiousness of speech and of the press may be abridged without lessening their useful freedom, and how far those abuses which cannot be separated from their use, should be tolerated rather than the use be destroyed. . . . That therefore the act of the Congress of the United States passed on the 14th day of July 1798, entitled "An act in addition to the act for the punishment of certain crimes against the United States," which does abridge the freedom of the press, is not law, but is altogether void and of no effect.[22]

Over the course of his life, Jefferson had expressed differing views on freedom of speech and the press. In 1787, he famously wrote that "[W]ere it left to me to decide whether we should have a government without newspapers, or newspapers without government, I should not hesitate a moment to prefer the latter."[23] In 1799, he saw the press as a protection against deception by politicians, arguing that a free press could be trusted "for light."[24] He also spoke in praise of free speech in his first inaugural address:

[T]he diffusion of information and arraignment of all abuses at the bar of the public reason; freedom of religion; freedom of the press, and freedom of person under the protection of the habeas corpus, and trial by juries impartially selected. These principles form the bright constellation which had gone before us and guided our steps through an age of revolution and reformation. The wisdom of our sages and blood of our heroes have been devoted to their attainment. They should be the creed of our political faith, the test of civic instruction, the touchstone by which to try the services of those we trust; and should we wander from them in moments of error of alarm, let us hasten to retrace our steps and to regain the road which alone leads to peace, liberty and safety.[25]

In that address, he also famously said, "We have called by different names brethren of the same principle. We are all republicans, we are all federalists. If there be any among us who would wish to dissolve this union or to change its republican form, let them stand undisturbed as monuments of the safety with which error of opinion may be tolerated where reason is left free to combat it."

But then, after Jefferson had served for six years as president, he felt very differently about the often-raucous American press, writing to a Virginia man named John Norvell that "the man who never looks into a newspaper is better informed than he who reads them: inasmuch as he who knows nothing is nearer to truth than he whose mind is filled with falsehoods and errors. He who reads nothing will still learn the great facts and the details are all false."[26]

Jefferson went on to outline—perhaps facetiously—how he thought a proper newspaper should be organized.

Perhaps an editor might begin a reformation in some way as this. Divide his paper into four chapters. 1st, Truths. 2d, Probabilities. 3d Possibilities. 4th Lies. The first chapter would be very short, as it would contain little more than authentic papers and information from such sources as the editor would be willing to risk his own reputation for their truth. The second would contain what, from a mature consideration of all circumstances, his judgment should conclude too little than too much. The third and fourth should be professedly for those readers who would rather have lies for their money than the blank paper they would occupy.

He proceeded to rail against the culture of slander, from which he had suffered during his presidency:

> Such an editor too, would have to set his face against the moralizing practice of feeding the public mind habitually on slander, and the depravity of taste which this nauseous ailment induces. Defamation is becoming a necessary of life in so much that a dish of tea in the morning or evening cannot be digested without this stimulant. Even those who do not believe these abominations, still read them with compliance to their auditors, and instead of the abhorrence and indignant indignation which should fill a virtuous mind, betray a secret pleasure in the possibility that some may believe them, though they do not themselves. It seems to escape them, that it is not he who prints but he who pays for printing a slander who is its real author.[27]

In 1814, Jefferson "deplore[d] the putrid state into which our newspapers have passed, and the malignity, the vulgarity and mendacious spirit of those who write for them."[28] He complained that "advertisements contain the only truth to be relied on in a newspaper." During his retirement, according to one historian, Jefferson "cancelled most of his newspaper subscriptions and eventually stopped reading them altogether, in favor of books. He quoted Benjamin Franklin as saying that 'when he was young, and had time to read, he had not books; and now when he had become old and had books, he had no time.'"[29] Jefferson had time to read books and write letters during his long retirement.

In his letter to Elijah Boardman, written early in his presidency, Jefferson expressed considerably greater confidence in the freedom of speech and in the power of government to prevent violence without compromising that most basic of freedoms. In this letter, as contrasted with those to Abigail Adams, he drew no distinction between federal and state governments, resting his arguments instead on broader defenses of freedom of expression. It was a significant letter because it seemed to express his personal, as distinguished from his structural or constitutional, views about freedom of expression.

It was also significant because it dealt with freedom of speech, rather than freedom of the press. Although both are covered by the First Amendment, there are important differences. Speech is more immediate and may have a greater emotive impact than the written word. It is more likely to incite immediate action because it provides less time for reflection and for the marketplace of ideas to operate. Perhaps because Jefferson himself was a writer and not a speaker—he gave few speeches during his long political career—and because he was the victim of attacks from the press more than from orators, most of his writing about the First Amendment focused on freedom of the press. Although he had experienced great orators—Patrick Henry, Samuel Adams, and John Adams among them—he seemed not to worry as much about the power of the tongue as of the press. I am aware of no other letter that focuses so sharply on the pure freedom of speech, especially from the pulpit, and that is as relevant to our contemporary concern about imams who preach violence and who—in Griswold's words—"run about and inculcate these crimes upon our children and upon simple ones."

Jefferson's response to Griswold, contained in his letter to Boardman, speaks to these current concerns more directly than anything I am aware of in Jefferson's large corpus of writings.

Jefferson's arguments with regard to Griswold cover political, as well as religious, speech. Although Griswold made his arguments in the context of a sermon, they were political in nature, as were Jefferson's counterarguments. They shed a somewhat new light therefore on the relationship between Jefferson's views of religious speech and his views of political speech. The historian Leonard Levy—who was without benefit of this letter—argued that

> Significantly, Jefferson never applied the overt-acts test to political, as well as religious, opinions. Although his own faith was deeply held, he was quite indifferent about that of others. In his *Notes on the State of Virginia*, which he began in 1780, he remarked that whether his neighbor said that there were twenty gods or none "neither picks my pocket nor breaks my leg." But political opinions could pick his pocket or break his leg: he worried about permitting religiously founded opinions "against the civil government"; he supported political test oaths; he denied civil rights to nonjurors; and he was ready to imprison carriers of "traitorous opinions" in time of crisis.[30]

The letter to Boardman casts some doubt on Levy's conclusion. It suggests that Jefferson explicitly rejected the "traditionalist" limitations on freedom of public expression advanced by Griswold and espoused a view closer to the one advanced by the "new libertarians."

The late historian Arthur Schlesinger Jr. has reminded us that "all history" is necessarily "contemporary history" because it is written by contemporary historians who are "prisoners of their own experience." He quoted Oscar Wilde as having quipped that "the one duty we owe to history is to rewrite it" and commended those "who seek to reinvent the past to make it relevant to the urgencies of the present."[31] These "urgencies" include the need to strike an appropriate balance between the rights of radical preachers and the need to protect their potential victims from terrorism. A generation ago, Jefferson's letter to Boardman—even if it had been in the public domain—might have escaped the scrutiny of historians. But as Schlesinger has cautioned:

> Concepts of the past are far from stable. They are perennially revised by the urgencies of the present. When new urgencies arise in our own times and lives, the historian's spotlight shifts, probing at last into the darkness, throwing into sharp relief things that were always there but that earlier historians had carelessly excised from the collective memory. New voices ring out of the historical dark and demand to be heard.
>
> One has only to note how in the last half-century the movements for women's rights and civil rights have reformulated and renewed American history. Thus, the present incessantly reinvents the past.[32]

Among the "new voices" that may resonate with some contemporary readers fearful of the impact that radical preachers may have on encouraging terrorism is that of Reverend Stanley Griswold. Though Jefferson's voice is certainly not new, his specific arguments against Griswold, as they related to terrorism, have now been thrown into "sharp relief" by the "urgencies of the present." The "historian's spotlight" should now refocus on the two-century-old debate brought alive by current events and by the discovery and publication of Jefferson's letter to Boardman.

Despite its importance, the Boardman letter had remained in the Boardman family, and not in the public domain, since Elijah had received it from Thomas Jefferson more than two hundred years earlier. I became intrigued with the story of the letter itself, in addition to its content and implications for our current conflicts.

4

The Provenance of the Jefferson-Boardman Letter

The history and provenance of Jefferson's letter to Boardman are part of its fascination. The letter was passed down from generation to generation of the Boardman family, many of whom continued to live in New Milford, Connecticut, through much of the twentieth century. In 1926, the early-twentieth-century historian Charles Beard apparently learned that the letter was in the possession of a Boardman descendant, one Dr. George H. Wright. Beard lived in New Milford, and Wright was apparently a neighbor. Beard purported to quote a sentence from the letter in a July Fourth message he published that year, but he apparently never actually saw the original because he did not quote it accurately, though the differences are relatively minor—one word, *but*, was omitted and the punctuation was wrong. (A period was omitted in one place, and a semicolon substituted for a period in another place.) Nor did he provide the context for the quoted sentence.

Professor Beard's grandson, Professor Detlev Vagts, is my colleague and friend. He told me that as a child visiting his grandfather in New Milford, he remembered the Wright family. He assures me that Beard was meticulous in quoting material. It is likely that Beard was quoting from a handmade copy of the original and that the person responsible for the copying made the minor transcription errors. Recall that the copy I was first shown was handwritten—probably before the advent of photocopying machines.

Beard's errors were repeated when Justice Louis Brandeis, citing Beard, quoted the same sentence in his concurring opinion (joined by Justice Oliver Wendell Holmes Jr.) in *Whitney v. California* a year later. Then in 1948, Justice Wiley Rutledge, in his dissenting opinion in *Musser v. Utah*, also quoted the same sentence from the same source with the same mistakes.

The error was finally corrected by Justice Potter Stewart in his 1959 majority opinion in *Kingsley International Pictures Corp. v. Regents of the State University of New York*, a censorship case involving the movie version of the D. H. Lawrence novel *Lady Chatterley's Lover*. In a footnote Justice Stewart correctly quoted the same words, this time with the correct punctuation. He did not cite Beard (or the prior opinions by Justices Brandeis and Rutledge), though it seems likely that he or his law clerks came upon the quotation from one of these sources. Instead, he cited the Jefferson Papers in the Library of Congress. The Library of Congress has a partially legible letterpress copy of the Jefferson-Boardman letter.

According to Martha King, the associate editor of the Papers of Thomas Jefferson project at Princeton:

Jefferson often kept letterpress copies of his own correspondence which he retained almost like a letterbook. These were created by pressing a damp thin sheet of paper against the original so that the impression from the ink was transferred to make a copy. He used this method of copying his correspondence until 1804 when he purchased and adapted a polygraph machine for his copying purposes. Many of these press copies can be found at the Library of Congress and the Massachusetts Historical Society, large repositories of Jefferson originals. [I]t is a much fainter and blurred copy than the recipient's copy now owned by Mr. Dershowitz.[1] [The letterpress version is reproduced in appendix A.]

Jefferson loved his copying press machine so much that he bought one for his friend James Madison, writing to him about it with enthusiasm in 1787:

Having a great desire to have a portable copying machine, & being satisfied from some experiments that the principle of the large machine might be applied in a small one, I planned one when in England & had it made. It answers perfectly. I have since set a workman to making them here, & they are in such demand that he has his hands full. Being assured that you will be pleased to have one, when you shall have tried its convenience, I send you one by Colo. Franks. The machine costs 96 livres, the appendages 24 livres, and I send you paper & ink for 12 livres, in all 132 livres. There is a printed paper of directions: but you must

expect to make many essays before you succeed perfectly. A soft brush, like a shaving brush, is more con-
venient than the sponge. You can get as much ink &
paper as you please from London. The paper costs a
guinea a ream.[2]

Jefferson then became equally enthusiastic about the
polygraph several years later:

I believe that when you left America the invention of
the Polygraph had not yet reached Boston. It is for
copying with one pen while you write with the other &
without the least additional embarrassment or exertion
to the writer. I think it the finest invention of the present age, and so much superior to the copying machine
that the latter will never be continued a day by any one
who tries the Polygraph. It was invented by a Mr.
Hawkins of Frankford near Philadelphia, who is now in
England turning it to good account. Knowing that you
are in the habit of writing much, I have flattered myself
that I could add acceptably to your daily convenience
by presenting you with one of these delightful
machines. I have accordingly had one made, & to be
certain of its perfection I have used it myself some
weeks, & have the satisfaction to find it the best one I
have ever tried; and in the course of two years' daily use
of them, I have had opportunities of trying several. As
a Secretary which copies for us what we write without
the power of revealing it, I find it a most precious possession to a man in public business.[3]

In writing his letter to Boardman, Jefferson used his letterpress machine, and so no multiple ink copies exist as there

are with letters he wrote using the polygraph machine. The resulting letterpress copy is unclear in places and not all the words can be made out, but enough are legible that one can be certain that the original is authentic. The original letter, and its envelope with a Jefferson frank, was kept by its recipient (Boardman) and then, by descent, passed to his family members for 205 years. In 1945, the letter was in the possession of Mrs. George Wright (Ella C. Wright) of Washington, D.C.—whose husband was Boardman's great-grandson. Mrs. Wright allowed the letter to be photocopied by the Princeton University Jefferson collection. In 1974, the original letter passed to Dr. Cornelius Clark of New York, who indicated that "he was not interested in selling the letter as it was addressed to an ancestor and felt that it should stay in the family."[4]

In 2006, the family finally sold it to Argosy Bookstore—for reasons I have not been able to learn. Naomi Hample, who sold it to me, said that the owner, whose middle name she believed was Boardman, was worried about its deteriorating condition and thought that no one in the family would give it proper care. The envelope was crumbling and the letter itself had some cracks, folds, and holes and had to be kept together by an adhesive backing, but every word could be read and the ink seemed stable. (I have since had it preserved archivally by Debra Mayer, a wonderful professional restorer who has assured me that it will last far into the future. She also discovered an 1800 English watermark on both the letter and the envelope.)

I tried to bargain Naomi down from the price she gave me, but she wouldn't budge. She knew she had me, and she was right. My son, Elon, smiled knowingly throughout the negotiation, realizing—as Naomi obviously realized—that I was not going to let this treasure get away. Finally, she

Th: Jefferson returns his thanks to mr Boardman for mr Griswold's sermon on religious freedom, inclosed in his letter of the 18th. of June. he had before recieved it through another channel, & had read with great satisfaction the demonstrative truths it contains. to the 10th. & 11th. pages however he could not assent; and supposes that the respectable & able author, finding himself supported by the good sense of his countrymen as far as he has gone, will see that he may safely, in this part also, go the whole length of sound principle: that he will consequently retract the admission that the utterance of an opinion is an overt act, and, if evidently immoral, may be punished by law of which evidence too conscience is made the umpire. he will reflect that in practice it is the conscience of the judge, & not of the speaker, which will be the umpire. the conscience of the judge then becomes the standard of morality, & the law is to punish what squares not with that standard. the line is to be drawn by that; it will vary with the varying consciences of the same or of different judges, & will totally prostrate the rights of conscience in others.

But we have nothing to fear from the demoralizing reasonings of some, if others are left free to demonstrate their errors. and especially when the law stands ready to punish the first criminal act produced by the false reasoning; these are safer correctives than the conscience of a judge. he prays mr Boardman to accept his salutations & respect.

Th: Jefferson

Mr Elijah Boardman   July 3. 1801.

Here is the letter in Jefferson's own hand. I found it, framed it, and hung it in my home. (An alternate title for the book was Finding, Framing, and Hanging Jefferson, *which is what Jefferson tried to do to Aaron Burr! See chapter 12.*)

80

agreed to throw in a small first-day cover commemorating the invention of the airplane. This my son wanted to give to my nephew, who is an amateur pilot.

I walked out of the store beaming. I couldn't wait to start researching my newly acquired treasure and learning everything I could about its history.

This is a portion of the original envelope with Jefferson's frank because he was president.

On my next visit to the shop I bought several old books on Jefferson, including three containing his letters to various friends and associates. I wanted to be able to put my letter into its proper historical context. (I also bought a book illustrating various Jefferson "tchotchkes," such as drinking mugs, pitchers, and saltshakers. I recently bought a hand-carved pipe in the image of Jefferson's face. My daughter thinks I've become obsessed.)

In reading Jefferson's letters to his many friends and associates—both for this book and for two earlier ones—I learned how important letter writing was to Jefferson and how his letters constitute the most important and revealing source of his philosophy. This great man of the pen wrote no actual books. The closest he came was his *Notes on Virginia*, which he wrote during the early 1780s and which includes many interesting observations on science. Jefferson also wrote an autobiographical fragment—when he was seventy-seven years old—that outlined his family history and his own early life. It ends in 1790 when he became the secretary of state for our first president. It is largely a factual recounting of events. Nor did he compose, as Levy has observed, any overarching theory or analysis of liberty in general or of freedom of speech in particular:

> In the thousands of pages of his published works there is a notable scarcity of extended treatments on a single subject. Insatiably curious, he knew a little about nearly everything under the sun and great deal more about law and politics than any man of his time. But in all his writings, over a period of fifty years of high productivity, there is not a single sustained analysis of liberty. He was pithy, felicitous, repetitive, and ever absorbed by the subject, but never wrote a book or even a tract on the meaning of liberty, its dimensions, limitations, and history.[5]

Jefferson's theories are represented in his thousands of letters, most of them concise and to the point. He was at his
best and most revealing when he sat down to correspond
with friends, political colleagues, and even strangers. In
1811, he wrote to his friend Dr. Benjamin Rush, describing
his life after retiring from politics:

> My present course of life admits less reading than I
> wish. From breakfast, or noon at latest, to dinner, I am
> mostly on horseback, attending to my farm or other
> concerns, which I find healthful to my body, mind
> and affairs; and the few hours I can pass in my cabinet,
> are devoured by correspondences; not those with my
> intimate friends, with whom I delight to interchange
> sentiments, but with others, who, writing to me on
> concerns of their own in which I have had an agency,
> or from motives of mere respect and approbation, are
> entitled to be answered with respect and a return of
> good will. My hope is that this obstacle to the delights
> of retirement, will wear away with the oblivion which
> follows that, and that I may at length be indulged in
> those studious pursuits from which nothing but revo-
> lutionary duties would ever have called me.[6]

Jefferson's letter writing played an important part in his
life, and when a correspondent—especially one he admired—
stopped writing to him, he expressed great disappointment,
as when Abigail and John Adams ended (temporarily, it
turned out) their correspondence with him:

> I receive with sensibility your observations on the dis-
> continuance of friendly correspondence between Mr.
> Adams and myself, and the concern you take in its
> restoration. This discontinuance has not proceeded

from me, nor from the want of sincere desire and of effort on my part, to renew our intercourse. . . .

Two or three years after, having had the misfortune to lose a daughter, between whom and Mrs. Adams there had been a considerable attachment, she made it the occasion of writing me a letter, in which, with the tenderest expressions of concern at this event, she carefully avoided a single one of friendship towards myself, and even concluded it with the wishes "of her who once took pleasure in subscribing herself your friend, Abigail Adams." Unpromising as was the complexion of this letter, I determined to make an effort towards removing the cloud from between us. This brought on a correspondence which I now enclose for your perusal, after which be so good as to return it to me, as I have never communicated it to any mortal breathing, before. I send it to you, to convince you I have not been wanting either in the desire, or the endeavor to remove this misunderstanding. Indeed, I thought it highly disgraceful to us both, as indicating minds not sufficiently elevated to prevent a public competition from affecting our personal friendship. I soon found from the correspondence that conciliation was desperate, and yielding to an intimation in her last letter, I ceased from further explanation.

I have gone, my dear friend, into these details, that you might know everything which had passed between us, might be fully possessed of the state of facts and dispositions, and judge for yourself whether they admit a revival of that friendly intercourse for which you are so kindly solicitous. I shall certainly not be wanting in anything on my part which may second your efforts, which will be the easier with me, inasmuch as I do not entertain a sentiment of Mr. Adams, the expression of which could give him reasonable offence. And I submit the whole to yourself, with the assurance, that whatever be the issue, my friendship and respect for yourself will remain unaltered and unalterable.[7]

To understand Jefferson—to get inside his head—is to read and place in context his letters. Jefferson understood how important his letters, and those of his contemporaries, would be to understanding the early history of our nation.[8] As he wrote to William Short in 1816, "The letters I have written while in public office are in fact memorials of the transactions with which I have been associated, and may at a future day furnish something to the historian."[9]

He elaborated his views in subsequent letters to William Johnson in 1823:

Altho' I had not time to prepare anything express, my letters (all preserved) will furnish the daily occurrences and views from my return from Europe in 1790, till I retired finally from office. These will command more conviction than anything I could have written after my retirement; no day having ever passed during that period without a letter to somebody, written too in the moment, and in the warmth and freshness of fact and feeling they will carry internal evidence that what they breathe is genuine. Selections from these after my death, may come out successively as the maturity of circumstances may render their appearances seasonable. . . . History may distort truth, and will distort it for a time, by the superior efforts at justification of those who are conscious of needing it most. Nor will the opening scenes of our present government be seen in their true aspect until the letters of the day, now held in private hoards, shall be broken up and laid open to public view.[10]

John Adams, too, expressed the "hope one day your [Jefferson's] letters will be all published in volumes; they will not always appear Orthodox, or liberal in politics; but they will exhibit a Mass of Taste, Sense, Literature and Science, presented in a sweet simplicity and a neat elegance of Style, which will be read with delight in future ages."[11]

Because of the importance of Jefferson's letters—both to him and to history—I have decided to offer a seminar to first-year Harvard Law School students called "The Letters of Thomas Jefferson." We will read hundreds of his letters relating to the Constitution, to law, and to political philosophy in an effort to understand better the American legal system.

Jefferson's letter to Elijah Boardman, written "while in public office" and expressing his disagreement with an important and widely circulated sermon on freedom of expression by a prominent clergyman, "may furnish something to the historian" and anyone else interested in the views of one of our most significant founding fathers. It was held "in private hoards" for more than two hundred years and is now being "laid open to public view" so that it can "be read with delight." Jefferson obviously wrote his letter to Boardman (and preserved his letterprint copy) with the expectation that it would eventually be published for historians to study and for all to read.

As far as I know, the Boardman letter in its entirety has never been published. It is appearing in full, and in context, for the first time in this book.[12]

The significance of the Jefferson letter can be fully appreciated only if it is placed in its historical setting. In the coming chapters, I will first describe the general context and then address the five major intellectual arguments contained in the letter. These arguments, in the order they are presented by Jefferson, are as follows.

Jefferson first asks Reverend Griswold to "retract" his view that "the utterance of an opinion is an overt act," which, "if evidently immoral," can "be punished by law." He suggests that Griswold "may safely go the whole length" of the sound "principle" that opinions should not be punished whether merely held or publicly expressed.

Jefferson's second point is a practical argument in support of his first. He asserts that if an immoral opinion can be punished, then "evidence too *conscience* [emphasis in original] is made the umpire." But whose conscience? Jefferson implicitly asks. His answer is that in practice, it will be that of the judge. He then goes on to argue that if the conscience of each judge becomes "the umpire," the law "will vary with the varying consciences of the same or different judges." And if this were to become "the standard of morality and, and the law"—if "the line is to be drawn" differently in each case, depending on the particular morality of the judge—then this would "totally prostrate the rights of conscience in others."

Before we move on to Jefferson's third point, let me spend a moment on his choice of words in making this second argument. When I first read the original of the letter, I could not make out the word *umpire*, which appears twice. Jefferson's *r*'s look like *s*'s and his *p* looks like it is followed by an *r*.

The word, on first reading, appeared to be something like *umprise* or perhaps *comprise*. It did not occur to me that it could be *umpire*, since I think of that word more in terms of a modern reference to baseball. But a check of the dictionary quickly revealed that the word has been in common

At first, I wasn't sure that I had read this word right—I thought it said umpire, *as in baseball, but I figured that could not be the case, because baseball as we know it was invented decades later. As it turns out, it was indeed* umpire. *The word dates back to before Jefferson's time, coming from the Latin* non par, *meaning not equal; it came into its current meaning in French during the 1400s.*

usage for centuries, deriving from the Latin *non par*—or "not equal." The "n" was dropped and the word became *umpire*, meaning a person who was above the fray, or a judge. Jefferson used it somewhat metaphorically to describe the criterion for judgment with regard to the immorality of an expressed opinion. In another letter, to Francis Gilmer, dated June 7, 1816, he used the same word in a different form: "No man having a natural right to be the judge between himself and another, it is his natural duty to submit to the umpirage of an impartial third."[13]

One other word caught my attention. Jefferson refers to "evidence too conscience." Today the middle word would be spelled *to*, not *too*. I initially assumed Jefferson had made a simple spelling (or homophone) error,[14] but then I came upon a letter he had written to his young daughter Martha, in which he urged her to "take care that you never spell a word wrong. Always before you write a word consider how it is spelt, and if you do not remember it, turn to a dictionary. It produces great praise to a lady to spell well." The editors of a book of Jefferson's political writing point out, however, that

> Jefferson, alas, did not follow his own advice. His spelling is often unusual, not to say idiosyncratic, even by eighteenth-century standards. For example, he writes "it's" when we would write "its"—as in "the tree of liberty must be refreshed from time to time with the blood of patriots and tyrants. It is it's [*sic*] natural manure." He sometimes drops letters that we expect to see, as when he writes "knoledge" instead of knowledge, and substitutes one for another, as in "scull" for skull. And he often abbreviates words, e.g. "govt" for government, "consn" for constitution, and the like.[15]

In his letter to Boardman, Jefferson also misspelled *received*, spelling it *recieved*. I didn't catch the mistake myself because I, too, am a terrible speller who often confuses the *i* before *e* except after *c* rule. (As Mark Twain once quipped, "I don't give a damn for a man that can only spell a word one way.") Jefferson, however, had a better excuse than I do, because in his day—before Noah Webster published his first dictionary in 1806—spelling in the United States was anything but uniform. Webster's "speller," published in 1783, was intended to change this, but it took time, as evidenced by Jefferson's errors. Nor was Jefferson overly concerned with proper grammar, as he wrote in 1823: "Nor am I a friend to a scrupulous purism of style. I readily sacrifice the niceties of syntax to euphony and strength. It is by boldly neglecting the rigorisms of grammar that Tacitus has made himself the strongest writer in the world. The Hypercritics call him barbarous; but I should be sorry to exchange his barbarisms for their wire-drawn purisms."[16]

Jefferson became one of "the strongest writer[s]" in America because of his own preference for "euphony and strength" over the "rigorisms of grammar."

Let us return to Jefferson's arguments. His third point is that "we have nothing to fear from the demoralizing reasoning of some, if others are left to demonstrate their errors. . . ." This is the classic "marketplace of ideas" rationale for freedom of speech that Supreme Court Justice Oliver Wendell Holmes would seek to constitutionalize more than a hundred years later. As Holmes elaborated the argument in *Abrams v. United States:*

> [W]hen men have realized that time has upset many fighting faiths, they may come to believe even more than they believe the very foundations of their own conduct that the ultimate good desired is better reached by free trade in ideas—that the best test of truth is the power of the thought to get itself accepted in the competition of the market, and that truth is the only ground upon which their wishes safely can be carried out. That at any rate is the theory of our Constitution. It is an experiment, as all life is an experiment. Every year if not every day we have to wager our salvation upon some prophecy based upon imperfect knowledge.[17]

The marketplace of ideas is an empirical argument that history and experience have challenged over time. Jefferson bolstered his previous argument by offering a fourth point. This one is factual: "The law stands ready to punish *the first criminal act* produced by the false reasoning." (Emphasis in original.) His fifth and final argument is in the form of an assurance that "these are safer correctives than the conscience of a judge."

These five points remain controversial today, especially in the context of incitements to imminent harm that are not always amenable to response in the marketplace of ideas.

In the next part of this book, I will write my own letter to Jefferson, in response to his five arguments, thus bringing this important dialogue between Reverend Griswold and President Jefferson into the twenty-first century.

There is, of course, always the danger of reading too much into one letter. That is why context is so important. I will try to place the words Jefferson used in his letter to Boardman into the broader intellectual setting of his age. For example, the "overt act" requirement, to which he refers, is part of a more general philosophical movement of which he was a part. The historian Leonard Levy, as previously cited, has written that "the new libertarians," in Jefferson's day, "advocated that only 'injurious conduct,' as manifested by 'overt acts' or deeds, rather than words, might be criminally redressable."[18] Those who pressed this "absolute interpretation of the First Amendment" insisted that freedom of expression, "like chastity, was either 'absolute' or did not exist."[19] Levy disputed the assertion

> that Jefferson was an absolutist with respect to freedom of mind and spirit. One's thoughts and feelings raise no issues until they find expression in words and deeds. The question then is where to draw the line between the permissible and the impermissible and why. To speak of absolute freedom of the mind and spirit, unaccompanied by "free exercise," is a dodge and a sham.

When in 1651 the Reverend John Clarke was convicted in Massachusetts for preaching Baptist doctrine, contrary to the law's prohibition, he was told, "The court sentenced you not for your judgment and conscience, but for matter of fact in practice." In other words, the court acknowledged Clarke's freedom of mind and spirit. Yet he replied, "Be it so, that I say that matter of fact in practice was but the manifestation of my judgment and conscience; and I make a count that man is void of judgment and conscience, with respect unto God, that hath not a fact in practice suitable there unto." Jefferson would have agreed and, accordingly, devised the "overt-acts" test to protect the expression of religious opinion. What is significant is his failure to extend that test to political opinion. The "New Libertarianism" advocated the overt-acts test for political as well as religious opinions.[20]

Jefferson's letter to Boardman suggests that Levy may have been wrong about Jefferson's position. In that letter, Jefferson embraces a broad approach to freedom of speech and explicitly rejects Griswold's argument that the laws should distinguish between one's private thoughts and the expression of those thoughts in speech. Jefferson was unambiguous in this regard, and his words do not require much in the way of speculative interpretation.

On a more personal level, I come from an interpretive tradition in which a small number of words can produce volumes of exegesis. My name, Dershowitz, I am told by an uncle who is a distinguished rabbi, may derive from the Hebrew words *doresh, drash, darshan,* or *midrash,* which represent one of several levels of interpretation of sacred texts in Jewish law. As I explained the elements of this tradition in my book *The Genesis of Justice: Ten Stories of Biblical Injustice That Led to the Ten Commandments and Modern Law,*

> [t]he open-textured, often ambiguous nature of the Jewish Bible has fostered a rich oral tradition and thousands of commentaries on the biblical text. Within the Jewish tradition there are different kinds of biblical commentary: *pshat*, literal translation; *drash*, rabbinic explication; *remez*, symbolic interpretation; and *sod*, secret or mystical meaning. Jews love acronyms, and the acronym for these different kinds of biblical commentary is *pardes* (*pshat*, *remez*, *drash*, and *sod*), which means "orchard." The orchard of interpretation is supposed to contain the many faces of the Torah. Perhaps the most popular form of biblical commentary has been the midrashic Aggadah, on the biblical narrative and going beyond more text-centered *drash*.[21]

And so I come to the task of interpretation legitimately by way of my heritage. I also come to it by way of my profession as a lawyer and a law teacher.

Although Jefferson's words are certainly not sacred, his iconic status in the early history of our nation warrants a serious effort to understand the ideas he expressed in his letter to Boardman, even though it is only one of many letters.

I have not been able to find any response by either Griswold or Boardman to Jefferson's critique of the Griswold sermon. According to Martha King, the assistant editor of the papers of Thomas Jefferson, there is no correspondence with Griswold until November 1804. There is a record of several further letters between Jefferson and Boardman, but these have been lost to history.[22]

Although I tend to agree more with Jefferson than with Griswold, I will play the devil's advocate—a familiar role for me—and press Jefferson on his arguments. I do believe that Griswold makes some sound points to which Jefferson does not always adequately respond. I will begin by bringing Jefferson up to date on how freedom of speech has fared since the early years of the new Republic, and then will describe some of the problems we're facing today that might cause Jefferson to rethink some of his arguments.

PART
III

My Letter to
Jefferson

5

⸻⸺⸻

Where We Have Come
since 1826

Dear President Jefferson,

I recently came upon a letter you wrote to Elijah Boardman
on the eve of the twenty-fifth anniversary of the Declaration
of Independence. I realize that you wrote many letters during your lifetime (estimates run as high as eighteen thousand), having read some of them with pleasure, particularly
your correspondence with John and Abigail Adams, as well
as instructional letters to your nephew Peter Carr—in which
you advised him to read the Bible critically, even if "it ends
in a belief that there is no God"[1]—and your remarkable

valedictory letter on the fiftieth anniversary of the Declaration, just days before your death on July 4, 1826, in which you predicted that the Declaration would arouse people "to burst the chains" of "monkish ignorance" and substitute "reason" and "science."[2]

I found your letter to Mr. Boardman particularly compelling, because of my own deep interest in freedom of speech and because the issues you raise are still controversial and important more than two centuries later. I can easily imagine a variation on your argument with Reverend Griswold taking place today. Indeed, I would respectfully like to continue that conversation by writing you this letter, first bringing you up to date on what has happened in our country, particularly with regard to the issues you addressed in your correspondence with Boardman, and then discussing your important arguments.

The state of freedom of speech remains strong in our nation, even in this age of terrorism. It hasn't always been so robust, especially during times of war and crisis. You remember how the fear of an invasion by France—whether real or contrived—drove some of the same patriots who supported the enactment of a Bill of Rights to enforce the Alien and Sedition Acts, which punished precisely the kind of political expression that the First Amendment was intended to protect. You correctly regarded the federal sedition laws as unconstitutional and pardoned all those who had been convicted under them. You will be pleased to learn that your view was ultimately vindicated when the Supreme Court said that while "the Sedition Act was never tested in this Court, the attack upon its validity has carried the day in the court of history," citing "a broad consensus that the Act . . . was inconsistent with the First Amendment."[3] (I was a law clerk when that decision was rendered in 1964.)

This phenomenon of using fear as a justification (or an excuse) for censorship has recurred throughout our history. I don't have to remind you how John Adams and Alexander Hamilton used the fear of "Jacobins" and an invasion by France to justify enactment of the Alien and Sedition Acts, as I just mentioned, but this appeal to fear has persisted throughout our history. The Civil War over the issue of slavery that you predicted back in 1781 came to be. You wrote that if "something is not done and done soon, we shall be the murderers of our own children."[4] Along with so many children of both the North and the South, among the victims of this inevitable war was liberty. The great president who led the Northern states—a man named Abraham Lincoln—suspended the writ of habeas corpus and was rebuked by the Supreme Court. In both the North and the South, dissenters were punished for seditious speech. Lincoln's generals George McClellan, Ambrose Burnside, and William Tecumseh Sherman and Secretary of War Edwin Stanton harassed journalists, closed newspapers, and censored the telegraph wires and mail in and out of Washington, with some measure of approval by the commander in chief.[5] As Lincoln rationalized, "[A]re all the laws, *but one*, to go unexecuted, and the government itself go to pieces, lest that one be violated?"[6] These abuses weren't limited to the Union; despite the rhetoric of individual rights in the Confederacy, the reality was quite different, with pervasive orders of censorship that went well beyond legitimate "concern for protecting the secrecy of troop movements."[7]

During World War I in Europe and in the years immediately following, there were numerous prosecutions for the expression of unpopular opinions.[8] Deportations were part of the Palmer Raids, named for then Attorney General A. Mitchell Palmer. On the night of January 2, 1920, there was a "nationwide roundup of nearly ten thousand citizens and immigrants." These raids selectively targeted left-wing activists and members of labor unions for deportation— Russians and Eastern Europeans in particular, who were seen as a danger to national security. The raids "were noted for their conspicuous brutality and a virtual absence of due process." Indeed, in one such case a sentence from your letter to Mr. Boardman was quoted in a concurring opinion by two great Supreme Court justices. Many resident aliens were rounded up and deported for expressing controversial views.[9] Shades of John Adams!

Following World War II, a period of deep repression prevailed. It was called McCarthyism, after a senator who conducted witch hunts against anyone believed to be sympathetic to our enemy the Soviet Union. McCarthyism was similar in some aspects to the reign of intolerance under the Alien and Sedition Acts, which also targeted those who were believed to be sympathetic to our perceived enemy France. In both cases, the external threat served to rationalize legal attacks on domestic critics of those in authority.

Between the end of McCarthyism in the 1950s and the beginning of the twenty-first century, a golden age of freedom of expression prevailed, with few restrictions on speech and much healthy and cacophonous dissent. You would have loved it. Even some expressions that you might have deemed punishable were found to be protected by the First Amendment. Then on September 11, 2001, terrorism struck our shores, generating fear of more and worse.

Again, as before, the perceived threat came largely from aliens, this time Muslim and Arab radicals. Some of them were citizens or permanent residents of the United States. Others were not. But it was largely a "we-them" conflict. We, the non-Muslim and non-Arab Americans, were afraid of them, Muslims whom we feared might be terrorists. You will recall your own conflict with Muslim "terrorists" from the "Barbary" states who employed piracy—yesterday's terrorism—against American interests. When you and John Adams went to visit Tripoli's envoy to London, you were told that Islamic religious law authorized piracy. Here is what you reported to Secretary of State John Hay:

> The ambassador answered us that [the right] was founded on the Laws of the Prophet, that it was written in their Koran, that all nations who should not have answered their authority were sinners, that it was their right and duty to make war upon them wherever they could be found, and to make slaves of all they could take as prisoners, and that every Mussulman who should be slain in battle was sure to go to Paradise.[10]

These words have a familiar ring to my generation of Americans, who have also suffered from Islamic extremists who justify and incite terrorism as a religious "duty" and who promise "paradise" to those who die in battle with "sinners."

Ironically, it was an early instance of Islamic terrorism on the high seas that, according to several historians, persuaded many Americans of the need for a strong Constitution to replace the weak Articles of Confederation. Under the latter, it would have been impossible to raise the kind of national navy and marine corps deemed necessary to defeat the Barbary pirates. The *Federalist Papers*

> stressed the necessary linkage between trading vessels and warships. "If we mean to be a commercial people . . . we must endeavor as soon as possible to have a navy," Hamilton, the mercantile-minded realist,

maintained (*The Federalist* No. 24), and warned (No. 11) that without a "federal navy . . . of respectable weight . . . the genius of American Merchants and Navigators would be stifled and lost." Specifically referring to the North African threat, Madison affirmed (No. 41) that union, alone, could preserve the nation's "maritime strength" from "the rapacious demands of pirates and barbarians." Jay's private letters reveal an even more pugnacious approach. Arguing "the more we are ill-treated abroad the more we shall unite and consolidate at home," the secretary actually welcomed pirate attacks that would compel the states to rally against "the . . . dangers from . . . Algerian Corsairs and the Pirates of Tunis and Tripoli."[11]

The historian Thomas Bailey put it this way: "In an indirect sense, the brutal Dey of Algiers [the Islamic leader who incited and directed the Barbary pirates] was a Founding Father of the Constitution."[12]

Ultimately, you had to use military force against these pirates who claimed to be acting in the name of Islam. In the battle we are waging today against criminals who claim to be acting in the name of Islam, we, too, worry about the sermons being preached in a language we don't understand by imams we don't like—and who don't much like us. We are concerned that they might be inciting violence. It was almost as if the Reverend Stanley Griswold had anticipated the problem: "Suppose one of his simple disciples should commit murder, and it should appear that he did it in consequence of what this person had taught him on that subject; although perhaps it should not be sufficient to hang the teacher, yet it ought to subject him to some kind of punishment, and I think of considerable severity."

Many Americans today share Griswold's concerns. Some even would have little reservation about "hang[ing] the teacher," as George Washington would have done. He would have "exterminated" these "enemies to mankind" and "crush them into non-existence"—referring to the pirates and those who sent them in the name of Islam.[13]

In your letter to Mr. Boardman, you offer several arguments against Reverend Griswold's position. In the next four chapters, I will seek to engage each of your arguments in turn. But first an observation of why freedom of speech—as distinguished from some other freedoms—seems to be enduring today, even in the face of threats of terrorism.

Many rights and liberties seem to be subject to pendulum swings. When a right is seen by the public as having been taken to an extreme, sometimes a reaction sets in, and its pendulum begins to swing to the opposite direction. This may be part of a larger phenomenon that I have called "rights from wrongs," in which new rights develop from a recognition of historic wrongs such as slavery, genocide, discrimination, and other forms of brutality.[14] In a similar vein, you yourself wrote about a related phenomenon more than two hundred years ago: "When great evils happen, I am in the habit of looking out for what good may arise from them as consolations to us; and Providence has in fact so established the order of things as that most evils are the means of producing some good."[15]

Something like this seems to be occurring today with regard to the Fourth, Fifth, Sixth, and Eighth Amendment rights of accused and convicted criminals,[16] which reached their zenith during the period of the Warren Court from the mid-1950s to the end of the 1960s, and now are very much in retreat. In the minds of many Americans, expansions of these rights produced wrongs, and so now the rights are being contracted.[17] But this contraction does not seem to be occurring with regard to the rights of newspapers and more modern media. The reason is, I believe, obvious: suspected and convicted criminals, as a general matter, do not have the power to preserve their gains in rights. They have no constituency, no effective lobby, and little ability to present their case to a dubious public. They are generally despised and their rights not well understood or appreciated. Accordingly, they rely on elitist support from civil liberties groups, some judges, and a small sliver of the general public. When a large majority of the public demands restrictions on the rights of criminals, the courts tend to respond.

Moreover, when rights are accorded to criminals, the victims of crime are hurt. At least, that is the argument made by opportunistic politicians who wrap themselves in the banner of "victims' rights." The rights of criminals are seen, therefore, as part of a zero-sum game: rights for criminals cause wrongs for victims.

The situation with the media is quite different. They do have the power to preserve—indeed, to expand—rights once those rights are given to them. An apt metaphor for media rights is the one-way ratchet, not the two-way pendulum. The media use these rights to enhance their power. They can use their right of expression to persuade the general public that it is in the interest of that public to preserve, indeed enhance, the freedom of the press—that media rights are not a zero-sum game but rather a win-win situation. It is far more difficult, therefore, to take away or diminish a right once it is given to the media.

Consider, for example, the "right to be wrong." You once expressed the view—a view widely accepted today—that truth should be a defense to defamation. In other words, anyone should be free truthfully to expose faults on the part of another, especially a public figure. It seems quite remarkable today that it could ever have been deemed unlawful to truthfully defame a public figure, but that was the law for centuries.[18] As the legal historian Leonard Levy described the situation: "The legal theory at the time was that the truth of a libel made it even worse because it was more provocative, thereby exacerbating the scandal against the government, its measures or officials."[19]

You will be pleased to hear that your view has become the law today throughout the United States (and it is even beginning to spread to England).[20] But in recent decades we have gone much further than you suggested. In order to give "breathing room" for truthful criticism, the Supreme Court has interpreted the First Amendment to extend even to false criticism of public figures, so long as the falsity was neither deliberate nor reckless.[21] There is now not only a "right to be right," but also a "right to be wrong"! Moreover, the Supreme Court has ruled that under the First Amendment there is no such thing as a false opinion.[22] These rulings have been quite controversial because the media can easily destroy the reputation of good people based on bad information. Moreover, many in the media have abused this right and gotten away with it, as they abused their rights in your day. Yet there is no pendulum swing because as the media become more and more powerful, they become more and more difficult to rein in. This may, in the long run, be a good thing, but that is not the point I am making here. I am simply trying to explain to you why freedom of expression is so well entrenched in our country, even as other rights are subject to swings of the pendulum.

But how does this phenomenon explain the speech and religious rights of obscure and despised imams, whom the public regards as more like criminals than media moguls?

The answer is that the First Amendment does not distinguish between the imam giving a sermon to twenty adherents and modern electronic media giants, such as Time-Warner Corporation, reaching millions. A right given to—or not taken back from—Time-Warner trickles down to the local imam, the Nazi Party, and the pornographer.

That is why rights of free expression, once recognized by the courts, are difficult to rescind and compromise. Difficult, but not impossible, as the mid-twentieth-century history, for example, of Weimar Germany and the subsequent Nazi regime demonstrates. But, thankfully, we are neither Weimar Germany, nor are we ever likely to become a Nazi-like regime. Freedom of expression is well entrenched in our nation, thanks in large part to you, your protégé James Madison, and others of your generation.

Though the basic right of free expression remains secure in our nation, its parameters are subject to ongoing debates, especially in the face of terrorist threats. Such threats are far more likely to be exacerbated by oral incitements of the kind discussed by Reverend Griswold than by freedom of the press as practiced by mainstream media. It is precisely the freedom to speak immoral and dangerous words—the very freedom that you so eloquently defended in your letter to Boardman—that is most at risk. Let us now turn to your argument in favor of a maximalist view of free speech.

6

---·─►●◄─·---

Jefferson's First Argument

*An Expressed Opinion Can Never
Constitute an Overt Act*

Now, Mr. President, let me first turn to your argument that an expressed opinion—no matter how immoral or dangerous—should never be deemed an overt act subject to punishment. Reverend Stanley Griswold had argued in his sermon that a publicly expressed—as distinguished from a privately held—opinion could constitute an "overt act" and thus subject the speaker to punishment if the opinion might "influence others to do evil." You disagreed, arguing that the "utterance of an opinion," even "if evidently immoral," should never be deemed an overt act.

To begin with, the force of Griswold's argument is not fully met by your response. Griswold did write about evident immorality, but he then illustrated that elastic concept by reference primarily to the sort of immoral ideas *that might influence others to do wrongful acts.* It is not entirely clear from his sermon whether Griswold intended his examples to narrow his broader point about evidently immoral speech or whether he meant to include, as punishable, also speech that posed no risk of provoking criminal acts.

There is, of course, a considerable difference between speech that is immoral *in and of itself,* without regard to the potentially violent *consequences* of the speech, and speech that threatens to produce violent consequences. For example, a speaker might espouse the virtues of consensual homosexuality or of masturbation. You might regard such a speech as evidently immoral. (I know you regarded homosexual conduct as not only immoral, but criminal.[1] We'll save that argument for a different time. I don't know your views on masturbation.) But advocating such "immoral" acts is not likely to lead to violence, since the acts themselves are nonviolent. It is, of course, possible that nonviolent acts that are regarded as immoral could lead to violence on the part of some people who are offended by the act. We have seen that happen throughout history: peaceful civil rights marchers attacked by bigots; homosexuals attacked by homophobes; flag burners attacked by self-proclaimed "patriots." (My own definition of patriotism is closer to that of the writer Edward Abbey, who said that "a Patriot must always be ready to defend a country against its government.") In those situations, I think you will agree with me that it is the violent attackers, not the nonviolent demonstrators, who should be punished (even when the nonviolent demonstrators are awful people such as neo-Nazis or Klansmen, and the violent attackers are on the "right" side of the substantive issue). But getting back to my main point, surely you must acknowledge that there is a significant distinction between the expression of opinions that are merely immoral and the expression of opinions that are also likely to lead to harmful conduct. To be sure, Griswold did not limit his view of punishable speech only to that which would lead to violence. He included the expression of opinions "with the wanton view to *excite broils* and cause *needless dissentions,* or to influence others *to do evil.*" (Emphasis added.) Although his examples centered on specific crimes (and sins), such as murder, theft, robbery, cheating, and lying, his principle was somewhat broader and his line more inclusive:

> This, then, is the line I would have to divide between opinions, to separate those the teaching of which shall be punishable, from those which may be taught with impunity. On the one side are all those things concerning which conscience dictates something. On the other all those things concerning which she dictates nothing.

Good advocate that you are, you chose to argue against the broadest proposition put forward by Griswold, which is the most difficult for him to justify, without fully responding to his narrower but somewhat stronger contention. Though I tend to agree with you for the most part, I think Griswold's concerns deserve a fuller response than you accord him.

Let me explain why. First, a bit of general background on this issue. Historically, there have been two basic justifications (and several variations thereof) offered for the censorship of speech. The first is that the speech is immoral, offensive, or bad *in and of itself.* In a religiously based society, this concern is understandable. For example, one of the

Ten Commandments includes a prohibition against taking the name of the Lord in vain or making any graven image. (I know you don't approve of the Ten Commandments or believe that they have a divine source,[2] but I refer to them as a well-known example of expression that is deemed intrinsically wrong.) These forms of expression are deemed to be wrong *in themselves*, without regard to any evil *consequences* that may flow from them. (It's hard to imagine any evil consequences flowing from saying "God-damn" rather than what I was taught to say, "Gosh darn.")

The second justification for suppressing speech is that it will lead to bad consequences. Speeches that threaten to incite revolution or riot are prohibited because of the feared results of the speech. To show how far this concept can be taken, consider the old common-law rule that made it a crime to "compass the death of the king." *Compass* means "to think, imagine, or even dream" about the king being dead. The theory behind this prohibition is that thinking such thoughts could lead to doing such deeds. Even today, it is arguably a crime to talk favorably about the assassination of the president because talk can lead to action (as it did in the case of Israel's prime minister, Yitzak Rabin).

There is a long-established precedent in the common law against "compassing" the death of the head of state. In 1638, for example, the laws of the province of Maryland stated that "to compass or conspire the Death of the King, or the Queen his Wife, or of his Son and Heir" was an act of treason, "to be punished by Drawing, Hanging and Quartering of a Man, and Burning of a Woman; the Offender's Blood to be corrupted, and to forfeit all his Lands, Tenements, Goods, &c. to his Lordship."[3] In the seminal Blackstone *Commentaries*, the concept was explained and related to the requirement of an overt act:

Let us next see, what is a *compassing* or *imagining* the death of the king, &c. These are synonymous terms; the word *compass* signifying the purpose or design of the mind or will, and not, as in common speech, the carrying such design to effect. . . . But, as this compassing or imagination is an act of the mind, it cannot possibly fall under any judicial cognizance, unless it be demonstrated by some open, or *overt*, act. And yet the tyrant Dionysius is recorded to have executed a subject, barely for dreaming that he had killed him; which was held for a sufficient proof, that he had thought thereof in his waking hours. But such is not the temper of the English law; and therefore in this, and the three next species of treason, it is necessary that there appear an open or *overt* act of a more full and explicit nature, to convict the traitor upon.[4]

In the modern era, it is still a crime to talk in a threatening manner about the death of the head of state—instead of the king, the president of the United States. In 1969, for example, the Supreme Court heard the case of an eighteen-year-old convicted of threatening to kill the president, in violation of "a 1917 statute [18 U.S.C. § 871 (a)] which prohibits any person from 'knowingly and willfully . . . [making] any threat to take the life of or to inflict bodily harm upon the President of the United States'" (394 U.S. 705). While the Court overturned the boy's conviction—on the grounds that it was "political hyperbole" and not a serious threat—it did not overturn the law.

In April 2001, a Syracuse, New York, man was arrested and charged for threatening to kill President George W. Bush; on a tip from his coworkers, the Syracuse police searched his apartment and found a videotape of him brandishing an AK-47 and threatening to kill the president. According to the law, anyone who "knowingly and willfully otherwise makes any such threat against the President, President-elect, Vice President or other officer next in the order of succession to the office of President, or Vice President-elect, shall be fined under this title or imprisoned not more than five years, or both." According to the *Syracuse Post-Standard*, the man recorded himself saying, "'This is the death,' . . . [then,] as if speaking to the president, he said he would 'Bushmaster (him),' according to the plea agreement. Bushmaster Firearms is the manufacturer of a type of automatic rifle." He made a plea bargain, ultimately serving six months of electronic home confinement and three months' probation, as well as agreeing to psychiatric evaluation.

According to the man's lawyer, David Secular, an assistant federal public defender, "[He] never meant to carry out his threats. It was just a silly videotape that was not meant to be taken seriously or viewed by anyone else. He does realize he never should've uttered those words."[5]

Again, a reference to the Ten Commandments will serve to illustrate the lengths to which this approach can be taken. The Ten Commandments include a prohibition against *coveting*—that is, desiring. This prohibition is based on the assumption that coveting may lead to taking, perhaps by violence or stealth. It is akin, in that respect, to the common-law prohibition against compassing. Recall our former president Jimmy Carter's famous admissions that he had "lusted" after other women. In an interview with *Playboy* magazine in November 1976, he said the following:

> Christ said, "I tell you that anyone who looks on a woman with lust has in his heart already committed

adultery." I've looked on a lot of women with lust. I've committed adultery in my heart many times. This is something that God recognizes that I do—and I have done it—and God forgives me for it. But that doesn't mean that I condemn someone who not only looks on a woman with lust but who leaves his wife and shacks up with somebody out of wedlock. Christ says, Don't consider yourself better than someone else because one guy screws a whole bunch of women while the other guy is loyal to his wife.

Modern secular democracies do not criminalize compassing or coveting, but some do criminalize advocating, promoting, or preaching harmful acts. (All governments criminalize inciting violence, although they define the terms differently.) Some punish merely immoral, offensive, or false speech, such as denial of the Holocaust (the genocidal program directed against the Jews of Europe during the early 1940s), defaming a group, or even blasphemy.

There are, of course, categories of speech that fit under both alleged justifications. Pornography, for example, is regarded by many as immoral or offensive in itself. But it is also believed by some people to lead to violence against women.[6] Moreover, speech that may lead to bad consequences is often, but not always, thought to be immoral. The writings of nineteenth- and twentieth-century revolutionaries such as Marx, Lenin, and Mao are regarded as immoral by some and highly moral by others—depending largely on whether one approves or disapproves of both the content and the likely outcome. Even the Bible has been condemned by some—including your friend Thomas Paine—as immoral for its positive descriptions of genocide and its use (or misuse) to justify crusades, inquisitions, and pogroms.[7] But as the great early-twentieth-century Supreme Court justice Oliver Wendell Holmes Jr. once put it:

> Every idea is an incitement. The only difference between the expression of an opinion and an incitement in the narrower sense is the speaker's enthusiasm for the result. Eloquence may set fire to reason. But whatever may be thought of the redundant discourse before us it had no chance of starting a present conflagration. If in the long run the beliefs expressed in proletarian dictatorship are destined to be accepted by the dominant forces of the community, the only meaning of free speech is that they should be given their chance and have their way.[8]

Tyrants, too, have believed this and have censored many ideas over time as dangerous. In a religious age, in which the church had the enforcement power of the state, it was not always necessary to distinguish immoral speech from dangerous speech. Both could be banned. Galileo's ideas about the earth circling the sun were deemed both immoral, because they contradicted the Bible, and dangerous, because they threatened the authority of the church. But in the America that you helped to invent, church and state are separate— thank God for that—and ideas should not be censored merely because they offend some people or because they contradict the holy books of others.

In contemporary Islamic countries, visual depictions of the prophet Mohammed—whether in sculpture, paintings, or cartoons—are banned because they violate the religious morality of orthodox Muslims. In non-Muslim countries, they cannot be banned on that ground alone. Indeed, our own Supreme Court has a sculpture that includes a beautiful depiction of Mohammed, along with Moses, Menes,

Hammurabi, Solomon, Confucius, Justinian, and other law-givers. In many places, self-censorship has operated to prohibit the depiction of Mohammed (in political cartoons, paintings, and even operas) on the purported ground that it would be offensive to some people. There are efforts under way in England to ban the teaching of the Holocaust in schools because such teaching is deemed offensive to some Muslim students who believe it did not occur.[9] The actual reason these matters are banned, however, is that the publication of such images or the teaching of such history may lead to violence by those who are offended. (This is called the "violence veto.") Similar constraints do not operate against anti-Christian, anti-Jewish, or anti-Buddhist speech because there is less fear of violence from offended members of these groups.

In the United States today, for a group to succeed in having a genre of speech banned, it is generally not enough to argue that it is immoral or offensive. It must also be argued that it is dangerous—that it may lead to consequences that are legitimately the concern of the state. The current debate over pornography illustrates this phenomenon. (You surely must have been exposed to early forms of pornography during your stay in Paris.) While some people believe that pornography is merely an innocent sort of voyeurism, many are offended by what they believe is a deeply immoral genre of expression. Others believe that in addition to being offensive, pornography may lead to an increase in violence against women—more rapes and more spousal abuse. Still others believe that even if pornography does not lead directly and measurably to increases in rape and abuse, it may coarsen sensibilities toward women, affect marital compatibility, increase sexist attitudes, and contribute to other evils that may not be measurable or provable, but that are nonetheless real and felt by women in their daily lives.

In religiously based societies, the mere immorality of a genre of speech, such as pornography, would be enough to get it banned. In a more secular society, such as ours, proof of evil consequences may be required. Even if such consequences are required, many difficult questions remain. For example, it must first be decided what kinds of feared consequences are sufficiently evil to warrant preventive censorship. As Justice Louis Brandeis, a great twentieth-century defender of free speech, cautioned in 1927:

[E]ven imminent danger cannot justify resort to prohibition of these functions essential to effective democracy, unless the evil apprehended is relatively serious. Prohibition of free speech and assembly is a measure so stringent that it would be inappropriate as the means for averting a relatively trivial harm to society. A police measure may be unconstitutional merely because the remedy, although effective as means of protection, is unduly harsh or oppressive. Thus, a State might, in the exercise of its police power, make any trespass upon the land of another a crime, regardless of the results or of the intent or purpose of the trespasser. It might, also, punish an attempt, a conspiracy, or an incitement to commit the trespass. But it is hardly conceivable that this Court would hold constitutional a statute which punished as a felony the mere voluntary assembly with a society formed to teach that pedestrians had the moral right to cross unenclosed, unposted, waste lands and to advocate their doing so, even if there was imminent danger that advocacy would lead to a trespass. The fact that speech is likely to result in some violence or in destruction of property is not enough to justify its suppression. There must be the probability of serious

injury to the State. Among free men, the deterrents
ordinarily to be applied to prevent crime are education
and punishment for violations of the law, not abridg-
ment of the rights of free speech and assembly.[10]

You will surely agree that Justice Brandeis's reasoning is
correct for two related reasons: First, the value we (and the
First Amendment) place on freedom of speech is so great—
especially in the context of prior restraint—that we properly
demand that an extraordinary burden be met before the
government is empowered to censor; and second, this burden simply cannot be met by invoking minor dangers to
property that could easily be remedied, such as trespassing
or damaging the grass. Any contemplated governmental
action that restrains the exercise of core democratic liberties,
such as freedom of speech or assembly, will rarely be able to
satisfy the stringent burden of proving that the evil sought
to be prevented is so serious, and so difficult to deter, that
prior restraint is constitutionally permissible. In this area,
more than in others, we are willing to tolerate many false
negatives (speeches that we mistakenly believe will not cause
harm) in order to avoid even a small number of false posi-
tives (speeches that we mistakenly believe will cause harm).

There are, of course, obvious and important differences
between the stakes involved in ruining grass in a park and in
preventing a terrorist attack. The questions raised by any
attempt to punish dangerous speech—whether the danger
posed is grave, as it is with mass-victim terrorism, or trivial,
as it is with walking on the grass—are both moral and factual: the level of evil, likelihood, and imminence required are
moral (normative) issues, requiring democratic consensus;
whether these levels have been reached are factual (empirical) issues, requiring evidence.

The broader question of what constitutes the kind of "evident immorality" discussed by Griswold and you is purely moral (or normative). It is surely immoral to express an opinion that would predictably cause another to kill, rob, or rape, but this sort of immorality does not exhaust the meaning of the word. There are other views, which, if expressed, would probably not lead to criminal acts by others, but which might still qualify as "evidently immoral." For example, expressing the opinion that "the institution of slavery is good" would, in the view of many (even many in your day), be regarded as immoral. (I know that you did not believe slavery was good, but you also did not believe that immediately ending slavery was good. Your views on slavery were complex, as evident by the metaphor you used to describe it: "[W]e have the wolf by his ears.")[11] But the expression of such an immoral opinion would not lead to criminal acts, at least in most parts of the nation.

Another related example would be expressing a view that blacks, Jews, Catholics, or homosexuals are "inferior." (Your views on these matters were also complex. You did not regard blacks as morally inferior, but you did say that based on your observations, you believed them to be intellectually inferior—but you also hoped you would be proved wrong.[12]) These views, too, would be regarded as immoral by many but would not predictably cause others to take criminal action unless the speech was directed, in a provocative way, at those labeled inferior. Similarly, Holocaust denial is false and immoral and generally motivated by anti-Semitism, but it is not likely to lead directly to violence.[13]

Thus, the distinction between merely "immoral" opinions and actually "dangerous" ones is an important one, especially in a secular society where the justification for censorship—if there is any—should rest on preventing evil acts, not on protecting against immoral ideas.

The Reverend Griswold conflated these rationales for censorship in his sermon. On the one hand, he spoke of "evident morality," of "anything which conscience, or 'the law written on the heart' plainly condemns," and of "things concerning which [conscience] dictates nothing." These sound like genres of speech that are immoral in themselves without regard to their possible consequences. On the other hand, he also spoke of consequences such as murder, robbery, theft, cheating, and lying—as well as "broils," "needless dissentions," and "unhing[ing]" society "from its formulations."

In your response, you focused first on Griswold's broadest prohibition against opinions that were "evidently immoral" and that represented "the demoralizing reasoning of some." Let me now deal with your argument against punishing this genre of immoral expression. I will then turn to the more difficult point relating to punishment of immoral speech that is also dangerous.

7

⟢⟡⟣

Jefferson's Second Argument

*If Conscience Is the Umpire, Then Each
Judge's Conscience Will Govern*

Your second argument purports to be empirical, based
on experience. You begin it by saying that if the
expression of an "evidently immoral" view were to be punishable, it would follow that "in practice" it would be the
conscience of the *judge* and not of the *speaker* that would be
the umpire.

This is a rather complicated syllogism based on several
assumptions. The first was one expressly made by Reverend
Stanley Griswold in his argument: namely, that if a line were
to be drawn between unexpressed opinion and expressed
opinion, that line would have to be based on *conscience*. The
second assumption is one made by you: namely, that if

conscience were to become the criterion, in reality it would turn out to be the conscience *of the judge*, rather than that of the speaker. The third assumption—also made by you—is that each judge will have a *different* conscience, and the law will "vary with varying consciences of the same or of different judges." The final argument—which you assert follows from the first three assumptions—is that if the first three assumptions turn out to be true, "[they] will totally prostrate the rights of conscience in others."

The first assumption reflects your decision to focus on Griswold's broader argument to criminalize the expression of views that are evidently immoral, without regard to whether they are also dangerous. Under Griswold's narrower argument—that a society should punish that genre of immoral speech that might predictably "influence others to do evil"—it wouldn't necessarily follow that the line would have to be based on conscience. It could be based on experience, even science. A court would have to look at *evidence* that the views expressed are likely to lead to harmful conduct. It would have to apply *legal standards* to that evidence, such as the likelihood that harm would follow, the nature of the feared harm, and the appropriate burden of proof. These legal standards would be based on the conscience of the broader community, as reflected in legislation, common-law development, and constitutional considerations. The conscience of the individual judge would, of course, play some role in his or her decisions evaluating the evidence and applying the legal standards—it always does—but to a lesser degree than you seem to assume. (Yes, we now have women judges, despite your mistaken view that "ladies were not formed for political convulsion."[1])

Even if the line were to be based entirely on the "evident immorality" of the expressed views, rather than on their dangerousness, I believe that your argument is both too narrow and too broad. It is too narrow because there are many other areas of law—other than the line between speech and conduct—that are governed by the conscience of the judge or, in some instances, of the jury (an institution you strongly supported, having written that you consider trial by jury "as the only anchor ever yet imagined by man, by which a government can be held to the principles of its constitution").[2] One obvious example is the "reasonable person" test (in your days, the "reasonable man" test) in the law of crimes and torts. The jury is the initial umpire of reasonableness constrained by the trial judge and then the appellate judges. You make no complaint about judicial discretion in those contexts. Your argument is too broad because it is the genius of the common law to constrain the discretion of judges by developing general principles that govern particular cases. Thus, each individual judge is not completely free to define the reasonable-person test for himself or herself: the standard the judge applies must comport with prior precedents.

Moreover, there are areas of the law in which the personal conscience of the defendant is explicitly made the umpire. For example, the law of conscientious objection requires that the individual have a moral opposition to war. The jury and the judge are required to assess whether the defendant, in fact, actually believes in his asserted morality, without regard to whether the jury or the judge shares that belief. In practice, of course, a jury or a judge is more likely to accept the good-faith belief of another person if the jury or the judge shares it or at least finds it plausible, but in theory the focus is on the individual's conscience. There are other areas of law as well in which the good faith of the actor is the umpire.[3]

If it were true that every judge would become a law unto him- or herself with regard to a defendant's exercise of conscience, then it would follow—as you assert—that the law would vary with "the varying consciences of the same or different judges." It would not necessarily follow from such variation, however, that "the rights of conscience in others" would be "totally prostrate[d]." This would depend, at least in part, on the *nature* of the variation. If the applicable *general standard* were to be *repressive*, and some of the *variations* were to be more *permissive*, then the effect of the variation might be more, not less, freedom of conscience. As with biological evolution, variation is the key to change, and some change is for the better and some for the worse. During some periods in our history, variation among judges has constrained freedom, while during other periods it has expanded freedom. The law is more complex than your syllogism suggests. I do agree with you, however, that unprincipled variation among individual judges is generally undesirable and inconsistent with democratic accountability.

Your use of the word *umpire* brings to mind an analogy to a game we play today that derived from the English sport of cricket. We call it baseball. The home plate umpire in baseball has virtually untrammeled discretion to determine whether a pitch is a ball or a strike. Players are not even allowed to argue these discretionary calls. Of course, an umpire, unlike a federal judge, does not have life tenure, and if he persistently errs in calling balls and strikes, he will be fired. But within a given game there is no appeal from the ball and strike calls. The rule is different with regard to other determinations made by umpires. They can be appealed, initially to other umpires and in unusual cases up the chain of command of the league. The question that your argument raises is whether determinations of conscience will become, in practice, more like ball and strike calls or more like less discretionary determinations that are subject to review.

We have gone through various phases in our judicial history with regard to that question. During certain phases, appellate review of trial court decisions has been rigorous and consistent. During other phases, it has been careless and sporadic. Moreover, the nature of judicial review has changed over time. For example, during the period that we call the "Warren Court" (named after its liberal chief justice Earl Warren), the Supreme Court was generally a court of last resort for aggrieved citizens, often minorities, criminals, dissenters, and other disenfranchised individuals—against the government. Then the pendulum began to swing. Today, the Supreme Court has become a court of last resort for aggrieved government agencies against individual citizens who won in the lower courts. As the *New York Times* editorialized on July 5, 2007, "Chief Justice John Roberts's court is emerging as the Warren court's mirror image. Time and again the court has ruled, almost always 5–4, in favor of corporations and powerful interests while slamming the courthouse door on individuals and ideals that truly need the court's shelter." Since government agencies generally win their cases before the lower courts, and since the justices rarely grant review to aggrieved citizens, the docket of the Supreme Court has shrunk in size and there is less judicial review.[4]

This recent approach emboldens some trial court judges to apply their own consciences, political opinions, idiosyncrasies, and biases. More vigorous and frequent judicial review actually reduces, rather than increases, the power of judges to enforce their own personal preferences. The reason for this is that lower court decisions are generally less visible to the public, the media, and the academy than are appellate court decisions, especially Supreme Court decisions. When lower court judges are free to apply their own "consciences" to low-visibility decisions, these decisions often receive little or no attention. When appellate court judges review these decisions, they tend to receive more scrutiny and accountability. "Activist" appellate judges may actually tend to reduce the degree of total activism in the judiciary as a whole. This, too, is a complex phenomenon that defies simple analysis.

I completely agree, of course, with your overarching concern about giving judges the untrammeled authority to serve as umpires of conscience or expression, although, as I will now explain, I disagree that "we have nothing to fear" from untrammeled freedom of expression. I will then turn to Griswold's more compelling concerns—about dangerous speech that can lead directly to violence.

8

Jefferson's Third Argument

*"We Have Nothing to Fear
from the Demoralizing Reasonings of
Some, if Others Are Left Free to
Demonstrate Their Errors"*

Your third argument presents the classic marketplace
of ideas justification for freedom of speech: if the
marketplace of ideas remains open to all, then the "good"
ideas will drive out the "bad" ones. It is entirely empirical,
and it is—I respectfully believe—almost certainly false. The
argument presupposes that if all ideas are allowed to be
expressed, the marketplace will see to it that good ideas
drive out the bad. A variant on Adam Smith's invisible
hand—or perhaps what you believed was a universal "moral
sense"—is presumed to be at work. The problem is that the
metaphor to economic markets simply is inapt, and the existence of an inborn moral sense is questionable. (I think the

comedian Gilda Radner came closer to the truth when she said that "human nature is largely something that has to be overcome.")

History has repeatedly proved that bad ideas often drive out good ones and that the marketplace of ideas is at best highly inefficient. As one of our great twentieth-century statesmen, Winston Churchill, the former prime minister of Great Britain, observed based on his experience, "A lie gets halfway around the world before the truth has a chance to get its pants on." This observation is even truer today than when it was made half a century ago because technology is quicker, and fascinating lies are often more interesting to the media than boring truths are. You seemed to acknowledge that this marketplace can produce false beliefs when you observed that "the man who never looks into a newspaper is better informed than he who reads them."[1] But you may perhaps be excused that hyperbole since it was written at the height of the newspaper attacks on you.

Even if the marketplace were an apt analogy, in most markets the golden rule prevails: he who has the gold rules. Speech is not free in a market-driven economy; it is quite expensive. Even your friend Thomas Paine had to charge for his revolutionary leaflet "Common Sense."

With respect, I believe that your argument is part of a deeply flawed approach to civil liberties that prevails even today, among some absolutists. The absolutist refuses to recognize that we must often make choices among evils. Consider, for example, the debate about torture that is roiling the civilized world today. Many civil libertarians refuse to recognize that there is even a conflict between liberty and security. They assume—assert, pretend—that torture *never* works because a person under torture will *always* provide *false* information. If only that were true, it would immediately end any rational debate about the use of torture under any circumstances.

The reality, however, is far more complicated. Torture often fails to produce true and useful information, for the reasons correctly offered by civil libertarians. But it sometimes does produce such information, as evidenced by the fact that many members of the French resistance during World War II were caught and executed after their brave colleagues were tortured into revealing their whereabouts. No reasonable interrogator would ever *believe* any statement produced under torture, but that is not how torture works in barbaric societies (or even in less barbaric societies). The torturer does not seek *statements* from his victim (unless he is trying to secure a confession, and he doesn't care whether it's true or false). He seeks self-proving preventive information. "Take me to where the bombs are hidden." "Show me the plans." "Call your collaborator and tell him to meet you somewhere." We should, in my view, seek to abolish torture, not because it never works, but rather because even if it does sometimes work, the moral calculus applied by democratic societies should reject the use of torture, despite its occasionally useful results. That is the honest argument civil libertarians and politicians refuse to make. The reason they refuse to make it is that if they were candid, they would have to concede that they are willing to see some innocent people killed by terrorists, rather than to permit terrorists to be tortured.[2]

Civil liberty absolutists, in my experience, are often reluctant to acknowledge that they are making difficult trade-offs. There are few "free lunches" when it comes to civil liberties.

Virtually all complex moral issues require a choice of evils. Freedom of speech is certainly among them. I am afraid that you were wrong to argue that we have nothing to fear from the expression of dangerous opinions, if they are countered in the marketplace of ideas. First, there is often no market-place, only a monopoly. We have much to fear in such situations, as evidenced by the effect of Nazi propaganda on Germans and others throughout Europe, as evidenced by the impact of the incitements to tribal genocide in the African nation of Rwanda, and as evidenced by the effect that the speeches of imams have had on suicide bombers who are being used today against the United States and other nations. Rabbi Meir Kahane, the late head of the Jewish Defense League, certainly had blood on his hands for some of the speeches he made and the way he inspired young, naive JDL members to plant bombs. And he operated in an open marketplace of ideas. I know, because I was part of that marketplace, urging his young Jewish followers to eschew violence.

Freedom of speech should be protected not because the marketplace of ideas assures that the good will drive out the bad, but despite the reality that the bad will sometimes prevail. Free speech should also be permitted because the alternative is more dangerous. Any system of censorship must either be pervasive or selective. There can never be just "a little" censorship. The choice is between what I call "the taxicab theory of free speech" and a "system of censorship." Just as a taxi cab must accept all law-abiding passengers who can pay the fare, without discriminating on the basis of where they are going or why they are going there, so, too, a government or a university may not pick and choose between what speeches, books, or magazines may be offensive. Once it gets into the business of picking and choosing among viewpoints, then it must create a fair and equitable *system* of censorship based on articulated principles. If it decides that items offensive to some women can be banned, then it will have difficulty rejecting the claims of offensiveness made by blacks, Jews, homosexuals, fundamentalist Christians, atheists, vegetarians, anti-fur proponents, and other politically correct and incorrect groups. I call this "ism equity." Both alternatives—pervasive censorship and ism equity—produce terrible results.

A more powerful case for freedom of speech than the one you offered must acknowledge that speech can be dangerous, that it can cause harmful acts, that the marketplace of ideas is no guarantee of safety, but that the costs of imposing a regime of censorship outweigh the costs of tolerating dangerous speech and its consequences. Your "marketplace of ideas" argument would have been strengthened if you had said that we have *less* to fear from the free expression of ideas than we do from their suppression, rather than categorically stating that we have *nothing* to fear, so long as "others are left free to demonstrate their errors."

In an ideal world of rational thinkers, you may well be right. You lived in a world closer to that ideal than we do today. Your letters to John and Abigail Adams demonstrate the power of reason among the reasonable. You changed your mind on various subjects, as did they—based on reasoned arguments.[3] I'm afraid the world we live in today—a world dominated by shouting talk-show hosts, cynical image makers, crass opportunists, political pollsters, and leaders who govern by following the polls—is a far cry from the New England town meeting, the Virginia salons, or the Greek amphitheaters where democracy took root. And even in Athens, the ideas expressed by Socrates were greeted not by immediate acceptance but by hemlock. The marketplace of ideas—limited as it may have been in ancient Greece—did not protect Socrates, although his good ideas, or at least those that survived, have been accepted by the marketplace of history. Consider, however, how many good ideas died along with their authors—in the Crusades, the Inquisition, and the slave trade of which you were aware, as well as in genocides that have occurred since your death, including the Holocaust; the Stalinist purges in the Soviet Union; genocides in Africa, Cambodia, and Armenia; the Chinese "cultural revolution"; and other mass slaughters.

The ideas that the marketplace left to us may well constitute but a fraction of those devised by the minds of creative men and women over time. The marketplace of ideas is the best option for a democracy not because it always produces the best ideas, but because—like democracy itself—the alternatives are far worse. What Winston Churchill famously said of democracy—"the worst form of government, except for all those other forms that have been tried"—might also be said about the marketplace of ideas.

9

———=ﭯﻪﭯ=———

Jefferson's Fourth Argument

"The Law Stands Ready to
Punish the First Criminal Act
Produced by the False Reasoning"

Your fourth argument is that we can always afford to wait until the criminal act occurs before we punish. This moves the argument from merely immoral statements to potentially dangerous ones—statements that are likely to lead to "the first criminal act." It directly responds to Reverend Stanley Griswold's most powerful argument. Your argument in favor of waiting for the "first criminal act" is not, however, self-evidently correct, especially since you seem to equate "the first criminal act" with the first harmful act. (Otherwise, it would beg the question of whether a dangerous, but not harmful, act of speech should be made criminal.)

133

Many societies throughout history have punished inchoate acts—that is, acts that are not, in themselves, harmful but that may lead to harmful acts. Common examples include laws against speeding, drunk driving, and the unauthorized possession of guns. Indeed, even our own Constitution punishes the crime of treason. Treason is often inchoate. It is largely a crime of intention and status. For a person to commit treason, he or she must be a citizen and must commit an overt act manifesting an intention to wage war against the government. The overt act requirement was placed in the Constitution to preclude the new Republic from adopting the more open-ended British approach to treason.[1] Indeed, at common law, it was treason to compass the death of the king—that is, to imagine the king being dead. Talk about a crime of the mind!

Treason is an inchoate act because it is never punished if it succeeds. As Sir John Harrington famously put it, "Treason doth never prosper: what's the reason? Why, if it prosper, none dare call it treason."[2] A failed treason can, of course, be punished if it goes beyond inchoacy to action. You and your brave colleagues certainly understood that if your "treason" failed, you and your fellow signers of the Declaration of Independence would—in the words of Benjamin Franklin—"surely hang separately."

There is an enormous range of difference between punishing thoughts alone and waiting until the ultimate harmful act occurs. Along that continuum may lie a range of manifestations of intention and dangerousness, including planning, preparing, instructing, advocating, and inciting. You seem to conflate the concept of an overt act with the concept of a harmful act. But there is a difference: an overt act can lie on a continuum between causing absolutely no harm and causing massive destruction. In the middle of the continuum there can be a dangerous but not yet harmful act, such as buying a gun, planning an attack, or advocating violence. The laws of attempt and conspiracy focus on these midpoints on the continuum.

Your argument seems to beg an important question. If all that is necessary to create a crime is an overt act, as distinguished from a harmful act, why is the act requirement not satisfied by *the act* of *expressing an opinion*? That is what Reverend Griswold proposed. In the law of conspiracy, which in many jurisdictions requires an overt act, an act of speech can sometimes satisfy that requirement (though it is difficult to imagine how the requirement can be met by an act of merely expressing an opinion).[3]

I surely understand the desirability of requiring an overt act before a speaker is punished for expressing his or her views. I myself recently was subject to an investigation by an Italian prosecutor for merely expressing my negative view regarding a judicial opinion that had been rendered in Italy.

You can imagine my surprise when I opened an envelope one day and saw a notice that an Italian prosecutor in the city of Turin had initiated a criminal investigation of me. I had no idea what she could be referring to. The letter stated that I had committed the alleged act in the city of Turin on January 27, 2005. I checked my calendar and discovered that I was teaching students at Harvard Law School on that day and then attending a lecture by a prominent federal judge. I could not possibly have been in Turin or engaged in any overt act there. Yet I soon discovered that I was being charged with criminal libel for statements I had made in an interview with an Italian journalist over the telephone. The journalist was in New York. I was sitting at my desk in Cambridge. But the interview was published by the newspaper *La Stampa* in Turin on January 25, 2005. Accordingly, the alleged criminal act had taken place in Turin, even though I had never set foot in that city. Nor had I engaged in any overt act other than responding to questions and expressing my heartfelt views about a judge who had written a foolish and dangerous judicial opinion that ruled that three men suspected of recruiting suicide bombers were "guerrillas" and therefore not terrorists, and not guilty.

I characterized the judge's opinion as a "Magna Carta for terrorism," and instead of answering (or ignoring) me, she filed charges with the prosecutor, who was required to open an investigation. Since my views were neither immoral nor dangerous, even Reverend Griswold would not support punishing my expression of them. But what if they had been dangerous? What if I had advocated a violent reaction to the judge's opinion? Provided her home address? The routes her children take to school? A place to obtain guns?

Such *acts* of *speech* go well beyond the mere expression of opinions and thus raise far more difficult questions of whether and when such acts of expression are appropriately punishable. A distinguished historian of my generation, Leonard Levy, has charged you with failing to work out a "usable test" for cases involving advocacy of "political crimes": "It is significant, however, that he did not apply the overt-acts test outside of the realm of the free exercise of religion. It is even more significant that his literary remains show no evidence that he ever tried to work out a usable test for cases of verbal political crimes."[4]

He was wrong to say that you did not apply the overt-act test outside of religion. You did so in your letter to Boardman. But even if he was right that you did not come up with a perfect "test" for political speech, you were surely not alone in that failure.

Over the years, efforts have been made to define political speech crimes—to distinguish the expression of pure opinions from the expressions of views that may lead to dangerous actions. This distinction harks back to Reverend Griswold's confusion between expressions that are immoral, in and of themselves, and expressions that may predictably lead to bad acts. Though this distinction may be valid in theory, it becomes difficult to act on in practice. In the early 1970s I represented a radical professor who was jailed for making a speech in which he told the assembled students that it might be a good idea for someone to destroy a building that he believed was aiding the war effort in Vietnam, calling it "a good target."[5] He was quick to say that he was not "advocating" or "inciting" any such action. He was merely doing what professors do: expressing ideas. Needless to say, a crowd of students immediately attacked the computer center because they thought his "idea" was a good one and they decided to act on it.

Today's radical imams employ a similar line of circumlocution, speaking in metaphor, poetry, and symbolism. But their followers know what they mean, and some may act on it. There is no perfect solution to this problem. Any reasonable line will either be under- or overinclusive—perhaps both. Speech is too varied, too nuanced, too malleable to be subjected to clear lines and unambiguous rules that are capable of being easily understood and uniformly applied. As you wrote to William Johnson in 1823: "Laws are made for men of ordinary understanding, and should therefore be construed by the ordinary rules of common sense. Their meaning is not to be sought for in metaphysical subtleties, which may make any thing mean every thing or nothing, at pleasure."[6]

Reverend Griswold, in the sermon you criticized, used a nice phrase in making a similar point. He talked about the need for a line that is so plain that "he who runs may read it." It is because no such line is possible with regard to speech that your final point, to which I now turn, is so powerful and ultimately convincing.

10

Jefferson's Fifth Argument

"These Are Safer Correctives than the Conscience of a Judge"

Your final argument—your bottom line—seems to have been interlineated as an afterthought. Perhaps you added it after rereading the original letter. You wrote to Boardman that "these"—referring to the marketplace of ideas and the vigilance of the law to "stand ready to punish the first criminal act produced by the false reasoning"—"are *safer* correctives than the conscience of a judge." I note the subtle change of language in this final point. Previously, you were more absolute in your views: "[H]e may *safely* . . . go the *whole length*," "[w]e have *nothing* to fear," "[T]he law stands ready." (Emphasis added.) In this final sentence, you use words that are comparative, rather than absolute:

"[T]hese are *safer* correctives . . ." (emphasis added). Now I can agree with you completely. History has shown that the libertarian approach to freedom of expression is "safer" than any regime of censorship—certainly, in the long run. Whether history will continue to support this approach remains to be seen. We must keep open minds—as well as open eyes and ears—on this ever-changing issue and the challenges it poses in a world of mass-casualty, religiously inspired suicide terrorism.

In the spirit of reason, and of the open marketplace of ideas, I hope, Mr. President, that you will agree with me that the important issues you raised in response to Reverend Stanley Griswold's sermon deserve continuing reassessment based on changing experiences. You argued that even the most basic provisions of our Constitution should be reconsidered over time. As you wrote to Samuel Kercheval on July 12, 1816:

> Some men look at constitutions with sanctimonious reverence, and deem them like the arc of the covenant, too sacred to be touched. They ascribe to the men of the preceding age a wisdom more than human, and suppose what they did to be beyond amendment. I knew that age well; I belonged to it, and labored with it. It deserved well of its country. . . . But I also know, that laws and institutions must go hand in hand with the progress of the human mind. As that becomes more developed, more enlightened, as new discoveries are made, new truths disclosed, and manners and opinions change with the change of circumstances, institutions must advance also, and keep pace with the times. We might as well require a man to wear still the coat which fitted him when a boy, as civilized society to remain ever under the regimen of their barbarous ancestors.[1]

Although our Constitution has endured for more than two centuries, and with very few amendments, it has surely changed through interpretation and construction. The words of our First Amendment have remained constant— "Congress shall make no law . . . abridging the freedom of speech"—but their meaning has changed quite dramatically. In your day, the First Amendment did not apply to the states, which remained free to enact and enforce sedition, libel, and slander laws, even against those who criticized public figures like yourself. Today, the First Amendment is fully applicable to the states, and defamation laws may not be used as swords by public figures to stifle criticisms of them— except in extreme cases.[2] Both freedom of speech and the dangers posed by incitements to violence have experienced exponential growth.

You were entirely correct—and, as a sitting president subject to scathing verbal attacks, extremely brave—to make the case for the fullest freedom of speech. Reverend Griswold's view, taken to its logical extreme, is a prescription for a regime of censorship. You were right to press him to "go the whole length of sound principle" and to "retract" his proposed limitation on freedom of expression. But I am afraid that experience since the time you penned those wise words has taught a more nuanced lesson than the one you drew from your experiences. You lived in a world where censorship was the norm and freedom of expression an experiment. Naturally, you saw the dangers of censorship more clearly than the dangers of untrammeled expression of dangerous views. I have seen both. Yet I agree completely with your ultimate conclusion favoring a maximalist view of freedom of speech as the safer corrective. The difference between us is that I believe this freedom comes with a price, sometimes even a heavy price. But you seem to agree that it is a price worth paying—especially considering the alternative. As you presciently observed in 1788, "[T]he natural progress of things is for liberty to yield and for government to gain ground." We must resist such "progress" and struggle against the natural inclination to give up liberty for the promise of security. As Roger Baldwin, the founder of the American Civil Liberties Union, once put it, "[T]he struggle for liberty never stays won." We who love liberty can never rest.

May I close this letter by thanking you profusely for the legacy of liberty you left us and for the trust you placed in the people who would succeed you—a very different and more diverse people now from the ones you knew in Virginia, Philadelphia, Washington, and New England. We treasure your legacy and feel a deep obligation to the past to honor it, as well as a commitment to the future to adapt it to the new realities we face. Among these new realities is the threat of global terrorism on a scale you could not have imagined. Nor could you or Reverend Griswold have imagined the influence certain religious and political leaders today have on their followers—an influence that extends to making them willing, even anxious, to die in order to kill their enemies. They exercise this pernicious influence through the expression of ideas and opinions, and they do it on a scale unimaginable even a few years ago. There is a real question whether, with the increasing availability of weapons of mass destruction—nuclear, biological, and chemical—we will endure or even survive. I wish you were here today to help guide us through this thicket. I know your guidance would be wise and valuable. But your work is done. The rest is up to us and our successors.

There is a wonderful legend from the Jewish Talmud (which you, on occasion, cited) that illustrates the relationship between the lawgivers and those who must later interpret and apply the law. Although the legend relates to God as the lawgiver, it is also relevant to human lawgivers like yourself who are now gone. The legend concerns an argument over the proper mode of interpreting the Torah. The focus of the argument was an arcane law about an oven. To support his interpretation of the law, Rabbi Eliezer invoked the original intent of the author of the Torah, God Himself. Eliezer implored, "If the *halachah* [the authoritative meaning of the law] agrees with me, let it be proved from heaven!" God then shook the walls of the study hall, but the other rabbis refused to be influenced by walls. Nor were they influenced by the river changing its course or a tree falling. Finally, God Himself spoke with a heavenly voice crying out to the others: "Why do ye dispute with R[abbi] Eliezer, seeing that . . . the *halachah* agrees with him!" (Pretty authoritative evidence of the original intent!) But another rabbi rose up and rebuked God for interfering in this very human dispute. "Thou has long since written the Torah" and "we pay no attention to a Heavenly Voice."[3] The message was clear: God's children were telling their Father, "It is our job, as the rabbis, to give meaning to the Torah that you gave us. You gave us a document to interpret, and a methodology for interpreting it. Now leave us to do our job." God agreed, laughing with joy, "My . . . [children] have defeated me in argument." I can imagine you in some constitutional heaven, laughing with a mixture of joy and sadness, as you watch us struggle with your words in an effort to apply them to our current concerns.

It is now our responsibility to build on your legacy and to strike the appropriate balances. In doing so, I hope we will always honor your resolute commitment to freedom of expression.

With gratitude and respect,
Alan M. Dershowitz

PART

IV

What Would Jefferson Say about Terrorism and Freedom of Speech Today?

11

<hr>

Jefferson's Views on the "Terrorism" of His Era

These final chapters consist of my own words and thoughts, based on what Jefferson said in his day, about how Jefferson *might* have addressed current issues, especially terrorism, and how—with the benefit of having access to two hundred years of additional history—I think they should be addressed. I was tempted to write a hypothetical response, in the form of a letter from Jefferson to me, about his views regarding the current problem of imams who inspire, advocate, or incite terrorism, especially suicide terrorism. But because I believe that it is always speculative to try to extrapolate the views of long-deceased thinkers on today's issues, I decided it would not be fair to put my speculations into Jefferson's words—even his hypothetical words. And so here are my thoughts on this pressing issue.

The arguments made by Jefferson against Reverend Stanley Griswold resonate today in many of the debates about how to prevent terrorism by Islamic extremists. Jefferson himself did have some exposure to Muslim extremism, in the form of piracy, kidnapping, extortion, and enslavement by the Barbary pirates. In the effort to make peace with the pirates and their Barbary state sponsors—who implicitly backed their terror on the high seas on Koranic grounds— the Americans entered into the Tripoli Treaty of 1797. John Adams and Thomas Jefferson, fully aware of the role of religion in this pseudo-war with Barbary, explicitly stated in the treaty that the "government of the United States is not in any sense founded on the Christian religion." When all diplomatic efforts failed,[1] Jefferson sent in the marines. The success of their mission is enshrined in the marine anthem "from the halls of Montezuma to the shores of Tripoli"—the latter referring to the 1805 attack on what is now Libya. Although the Barbary pirates claimed to be acting pursuant to Islamic law, they were not suicide terrorists. They wanted to live and reap the material benefits of their predatory actions (though their leader assured them a place in paradise if they were to die in the struggle against the heathens).

Jefferson lived in an age when suicide was a sin (and a crime). The suicide killer was unheard of, except in biblical stories such as Samson and Delilah. Today, however, suicide is preached by some imams as an obligation and a step on the road to paradise. Suicide terrorists such as the ones who attacked us on September 11 cannot be deterred by the threat that they will be punished if they commit the criminal act of terrorism since they welcome the ultimate punishment.[2]

Preventive measures are thus the only realistic hope of stopping another 9/11—or worse. Some of the preventive measures that have been proposed—in Great Britain, France, Canada, Israel, and even the United States—include restrictions on freedom of speech.[3] Some such proposed restrictions would be limited to direct incitements, especially by religious leaders who preach to young, often isolated, and vulnerable co-religionists who do not have access to any "marketplace of ideas." These "simple ones"—some of whom are actually children—are cut off from the mainstream media, from popular culture, and from alternative points of view.[4] They hear only the most biased and false accounts of history and current events and are told that suicide terrorism is a religious obligation, a political duty, and a family honor. When a suicide bomber is selected and agrees to go forward with his murderous mission, he is deliberately isolated from all contact with family, friends, or anyone or anything that might give him an alternative worldview. Not quite the Jeffersonian model of the marketplace of ideas in which "others are left free to demonstrate their errors."

If Jefferson were to have been confronted with this very different model—no possibility of the terrorist act being deterred, no marketplace of ideas, the realistic possibility of mass-casualty attacks—would he have abandoned his absolute objection to punishing any expression of opinion, no matter how dangerous or "evidently immoral"? Would he still have urged waiting for the first "overt act," beyond the speech itself? What sort of overt act, short of the terrorist act itself, might have satisfied him? Would speech that involved directly inciting, commanding as a religious obligation, or even planning a terrorist act be enough to constitute an overt act?

Recall that Jefferson's arguments against Griswold's more censorial view were expressly conditional: "*if* others are left free to demonstrate their errors" and "*when* the law stands ready to punish the first criminal act produced by the false reasoning." (Emphasis added.)

Jefferson never expressly stated his views on whether bad people should remain free to advocate immoral and dangerous actions if these conditions could not be met. He did, however, express strong views on the supreme need "of saving our country when in danger," even if violating the written law becomes necessary. In 1808, he wrote to James Brown that "self-preservation is paramount to all law," citing the revolutionary acts of his compatriots in arms, which were clearly in violation of British law. He elaborated on the possible inadequacy of the laws in "extreme cases" in a letter to John Colvin in 1810:

> A strict observance of the written laws is doubtless one of the highest duties of a good citizen, but it is not the highest. The laws of necessity, of self-preservation, of saving our country when in danger, are of higher obligation. To lose our country by a scrupulous adherence to written law, would be to lose the law itself, with life, liberty, property & all those who are enjoying them with us; thus absurdly sacrificing the end to the means. . . . The unwritten laws of necessity, of self-preservation, & of the public safety control the written laws of meum & tuum [the distinction between what is mine or one's own and what is yours or another's]. . . . [The laws of necessity and self-preservation] do not go to the case of persons charged with petty duties, where consequences are trifling, and time allowed for a legal course, nor to authorize them

to take such cases out of the written law. In these, the example of overleaping the law is of greater evil than a strict adherence to its imperfect provisions. It is incumbent on those only who accept of great charges, to risk themselves on great occasions, when the safety of the nation, or some of its very high interests are at stake. An officer is bound to obey orders; yet he would be a bad one who should do it in cases for which they were not intended, and which involved the most important consequences. The line of discrimination between cases may be difficult; but the good officer is bound to draw it at his own peril, & throw himself on the justice of his country and the rectitude of his motives.[5]

And in 1814, Jefferson declared (paraphrasing Shakespeare), "It is the melancholy law of human societies to be compelled sometimes to choose a great evil in order to ward off a greater."[6] As Polonius says in *Hamlet*:

Your bait of falsehood takes this carp of truth:
And thus do we of wisdom and of reach,
With windlasses and with assays of bias,
By indirections find directions out:
So by my former lecture and advice,
Shall you my son. You have me, have you not?

Jefferson himself may have believed the nation faced such dangers and evils from the actions of his former vice president, Aaron Burr. We can perhaps discern some clues to what his attitudes might be toward the threats we currently face from his own actions during the prosecution of Aaron Burr for treason—a case that arose during Jefferson's second term as president.

12

Jefferson's Actions
in the Burr Case

I n his standard biography of Chief Justice John Marshall, Albert J. Beveridge characterizes the proceedings against Aaron Burr as "the greatest criminal trial in American history." Although many subsequent trials also lay claim to this title—the trial of the Lincoln and McKinley assassins, to name just two—Beveridge's conclusion is certainly plausible. Most other Western nations have experienced numerous great treason trials. The United States has been spared such transforming legal events because there have been few attempts to seize power by force.

The dramatis personae alone would qualify the Burr case as among the greatest in American history. The presiding judge was Chief Justice John Marshall, probably the most influential jurist in our nation's history. Burr's attorneys included Charles Lee Randolph and Luther Martin—among the most prominent lawyers and patriots of the day. At an earlier stage, Burr had been represented by Henry Clay. Among his supporters was the future president Andrew Jackson. The prosecuting attorney was George Hay, the son-in-law of James Madison. He was assisted by William Wirt, a future presidential candidate.

The prosecutors took their orders directly from President Thomas Jefferson, who tried to manage the prosecution from Washington, declaring publicly that Burr's "guilt is placed beyond question." According to biographers of Burr, Jefferson was the driving force behind the prosecution:

> Jefferson fussed feverishly over the disposition of the case throughout the trial. Whether in Washington or Monticello, he wanted full reports from Hay and the others. He gave advice, suggested procedures, and planned strategy either through his own communications with [Caesar A.] Rodney and Hay or through Madison.[1]

He went so far as to summon and interrogate potential witnesses—once in the presence of Secretary of State James Madison, who took notes.[2] No wonder the historian Leonard Levy concluded that "Jefferson did not turn the case over to the United States attorney, but acted himself as prosecutor, superintending the gathering of evidence, locating witnesses, taking depositions, directing trial tactics, and shaping public opinion as if judge and juror for the nation. The object was not to secure justice by having Burr's guilt—or innocence—fairly determined, but to secure a conviction, no matter how, on the charge of high treason."[3]

The political stakes were high for everyone involved. Despite Jefferson's strong belief in the separation of powers, the president let it be known that "if Marshall should suffer Burr to escape, Marshall himself should be removed from office."[4] And Marshall acknowledged that "it would be difficult or dangerous for a jury to acquit Burr, however innocent they may think him."[5]

It is easy to forget that Aaron Burr was a person of considerable stature. He will always be remembered in American history as the man who killed Alexander Hamilton in a duel in Weehawken, New Jersey, in July 1804. I have an old newspaper, the July 24, 1804, edition of the *Boston Repertory*, that reported "[t]he shocking catastrophe [that terminated] the life of Alexander Hamilton and which has spread gloom over our city that will not be speedily dissipated." It also reprinted the remarkable exchange of letters that precipitated the fatal duel. The very idea that a sitting vice president would duel a former secretary of the Treasury (and a potential future president) seems beyond our current imagination. Reading the letters makes the duel seem even more absurd. The insult that precipitated the duel was mild by today's standards, and even by the standards of contemporaneous newspapers and opinion sheets of that era. The insult was not even stated directly by Hamilton. It was contained in a letter by one Dr. Charles D. Cooper to a friend. The two offending sentences were the following: "General Hamilton and Judge Kent have declared, in substance, that they looked upon Mr. Burr to be a dangerous man, and one who ought not to be trusted with the reins of government. . . . I could detail to you a still more despicable opinion which General Hamilton has expressed of Mr. Burr."[6]

It was the second sentence, particularly the words "a still more despicable opinion," that provoked the duel. Hamilton apparently tried, consistent with his honor, to make amends, but Burr would accept nothing short of an abject admission of guilt or a duel. And so it ended with a duel. Burr fired at Hamilton and hit him. Hamilton either deliberately or inadvertently fired into the air. Hamilton lingered for one day and then died, as his son had earlier died, also the victim of a duel. Freud once observed that the person who first hurled an insult instead of a rock made an important step toward civilization.[7] Hamilton and Burr set it back considerably.

Burr will also be recognized as the subject of the most notorious treason trial in U.S. history. It is easy to forget that prior to these events, he was an authentic American hero, on the scale of Jefferson, Madison, and Hamilton. Born into the best of families—his father was president of Princeton University and his mother's father was Jonathan Edwards— Colonel Burr had distinguished himself during the Revolutionary War. He came close to becoming president, tying with Jefferson in the electoral vote and losing to him in the House of Representatives on the thirty-sixth ballot. Under the system then in operation, he was automatically elected vice president. He did not run for reelection, instead seeking the governorship of New York, which he lost. It was after this defeat—and in some ways because of it—that he confronted Hamilton in the duel.

When Hamilton heard that Burr had been nominated for the New York governorship, he went on an anti-Burr tear. "He accused Burr of using Federalism as 'a ladder of his ambition' and further warned that the Colonel wished to promote 'the dismemberment of the union' and to become 'chief of the Northern portion.'" Burr couldn't help but hear of Hamilton's insults, and upon his loss of the election, "years of calumny and spite directed at Burr . . . [and] Burr's disappointment . . . settled his wrath on the Federalist

Hamilton rather than on the victorious Republicans."[8] Following the duel, Burr became a fugitive with little money or political influence, though he was still vice president of the United States. New York and New Jersey had issued arrest warrants against him, which rendered him an exile from his home area.[9] He returned to Washington, however, to preside over the impeachment of Justice Samuel Chase, which led one federalist wag to note that it was "the practice in Courts of Justice to arraign the murderer before the Judge, but now we behold the Judge arraigned before the murderer."[10] Burr presided over the proceedings with distinction and shortly thereafter delivered his valedictory address to the Senate as his term ended. It was apparently well received.

Between 1805 and 1806, Burr traveled through the South on a mysterious journey that became the subject of the controversial treason charges. Spending considerable time in the newly acquired western territories of Louisiana and Mississippi, Burr met with several different individuals with whom he allegedly hatched a conspiracy to conquer some of the territories—perhaps even Mexico—and thereby regain his lost political power. At the beginning of 1807, based on information gathered from Burr's correspondence allegedly showing that he had begun preparations for a large-scale military expedition, the former vice president was arrested in Louisiana and indicted on the charge of "wickedly devising and intending the peace and tranquility of the . . . United States to disturb, and to stir, move, and excite insurrection, rebellion and war against the said United States."[11] (These words could have been written by Reverend Stanley Griswold, who, you will recall, would have punished the expression of "wanton" views that "excite broils," "cause needless dissentions," or "influence others to do evil.") The indictment focused on a particular meeting "at a certain place called and known by the name of Blannerhassett's island," a private piece of land in the middle of the Ohio River where Burr allegedly made plans and contracted for supplies for a large-scale military expedition. No such expedition actually took place (though there was some disputed evidence of preliminary actions having been taken). And so Burr was charged essentially for what he said and planned. It was an inchoate crime.

Jefferson expressed his views regarding Burr to Monsieur DuPont De Nemours on July 14, 1807:

> Burr's conspiracy has been one of the most flagitious [an old word for shameful, vicious, scandalous] of which history will ever furnish an example. He had combined the objects of separating the western States from us, of adding Mexico to them, and of placing himself at their head. But he who could expect to effect such objects by the aid of American citizens, must be perfectly ripe for Bedlam. Yet although there is not a man in the United States who is not satisfied of the depth of his guilt, such are the jealous provisions of our laws in favor of the accused, and against the accuser, that I question if he can be convicted. Out of the forty-eight jurors who are to be summoned, he has a right to choose the twelve who are to try him, and if any one of the twelve refuses to concur in finding him guilty, he escapes. This affair has been a great confirmation in my mind of the innate strength of the form of our government. He had probably induced near a thousand men to engage with him, but making them believe the government connived at it. A proclamation alone, by undeceiving them, so completely disarmed him. The first enterprise was to have been the seizure of New

Orleans, which he supposed would powerfully bridle the country above, and place him at the door of Mexico. It has given me infinite satisfaction that not a single native Creole of Louisiana, and but one American, settled there before the delivery of the country to us, were in his interest. His partisans there were made up of fugitives from justice, or from their debts. Who had flocked there from other parts of the United States, after the delivery of the country, and of adventurers and speculators of all description.[12]

Jefferson had previously characterized Burr as a man of "overrated talent,"[13] reminding me of Teddy Roosevelt's description of John Tyler: "He has been called a mediocre man; but that is unwarranted flattery. He was a politician of monumental littleness."[14] Unlike Tyler, however, Burr had real impact on American history, as the result both of his dual with Hamilton and his trial for treason.

Burr's biographer, James Parton, writing in 1857, argued that Jefferson overstated the threat posed by Burr. He first quotes one of Jefferson's more exaggerated portrayals of the alleged conspiracy:

"Burr's enterprise," wrote Jefferson, January 11th, "is the most extraordinary since the days of Don Quixote. It is so extravagant that those who know his understanding would not believe it if the proofs admitted doubt. He has meant to place himself on the throne of Montezuma, and extend his empire to the Alleghany [sic], seizing on New Orleans as the instrument of compulsion for our western States."

Parton then goes on to ridicule Jefferson's characterization:

How nonsensical is this! What impossibilities does this closet-wise man attribute to his late companion and rival! By what means imaginable could the western States be *compelled* to yield submission to a usurper at New Orleans? The States of this Union are so constituted and circumstanced, the treason of the kind attributed to Aaron Burr is a simple and manifest impossibility! There is no part of Jefferson's long and glorious career in which he appears to so little advantage as during the period we are now considering.

In one word, the real prosecutor of Aaron Burr, throughout this business, was Thomas Jefferson, President of the United States, who was made president of the United States by Aaron Burr's tact and vigilance, and who was able therefore to wield against Aaron Burr the power and resources of the United States.

Parton, a Burr partisan, concluded that:

It was not without truth, then, that Colonel Burr wrote in the early stages of the trial:

"The most indefatigable industry is used by the agents of government, and they have money at command without stint. If I were possessed of the same means, I could not only foil the prosecutors, but render them ridiculous and infamous. The democratic papers teem with abuse against me and my counsel; and even against the Chief Justice. Nothing is left undone or unsaid which can tend to prejudice the public mind, and produce a conviction without evidence. The machinations of this description which were used against Moreau in France were treated in this country with indignation. They are practiced against me in a still more impudent degree, not only with impunity, but with applause; and the authors and abettors suppose, with reason, that they are acquiring favor with the administration."[15]

Burr's trial opened in Richmond, Virginia, in August 1807 amid considerable fanfare. It was certainly the greatest trial the new republic had so far experienced. The court proceedings against Burr could constitute an entire course in criminal law, constitutional law, evidence, or early-nineteenth-century American history. The opinions of Chief Justice Marshall, on subjects ranging from the definition of treason to the power of the judiciary to subpoena the president, to the scope of the privilege against self-incrimination, to the rules of evidence are among the formative judicial decisions of our nation's history. The proceedings from beginning to end comprised a political trial in the most literal meaning of that much-overused term. This trial was motivated by politics; it was about politics; it was argued as politics; the sides were chosen along political lines; and it may have been decided on political considerations. Andrew Jackson said it "assumed the shape of a political persecution."[16] Yet the law—at least, the structure of the law—played a significant role.

In light of the political nature of the case and the president's widely publicized declaration of Burr's certain guilt, it was obviously difficult to select an unbiased jury. Burr acknowledged that it would be nearly impossible to find twelve jurors who did not come to the case with prejudgment. He was prepared to accept jurors who believed he was guilty, as long as they were open to persuasion. He, too, believed in the marketplace of ideas—even in a courtroom where evidentiary rules limit the openness of the market. In fact, he accepted a juror who stated the following under oath:

I, too, feel myself disqualified for passing impartially between the United States and Aaron Burr. From the documents that I have seen, particularly the depositions of Generals Wilkinson and Eaton, I have believed, and do still believe, that his intentions were hostile to the peace and safety of the United States; in short, that he had intended to subvert the government of the United States. It would be inflicting a wound on my own bosom to be compelled to serve under my present impressions.[17]

Burr, who acted largely as his own lawyer in the jury selection process, responded to this candid statement as follows: "Notwithstanding Mr. [John M.] Sheppard's impressions, I could rely upon his integrity and impartiality."

When another prospective juror was called, he stated that he had conceived and expressed an opinion that the designs of Colonel Burr were always enveloped in mystery, and were inimical to the United States, and when informed by the public prints that he was descending to the river with an armed force, he had felt as every friend of his country ought to feel. The following exchange then occurred:

MR. BURR: If, sir, you have completely prejudiced my case—

MR. HENRY E. COLEMAN: I have not. I have not seen the evidence.

MR. BURR: That is enough, sir. You are *elected*.[18]

As it turned out, the most important rulings of the court were those excluding evidence of a treasonous conspiracy. A few weeks into the trial, Burr interrupted the prosecution's case with a motion to preclude any testimony about Burr's actions and conduct in the days following the alleged meeting on Blennerhassett's Island. He argued that the prosecution had "utterly failed to prove any *overt act* of war had been committed" and had even conceded that Burr "was more than one hundred miles distant from the place where the overt act is charged to have been committed"(emphasis added). In other words, Burr essentially paraphrased the argument made by Jefferson in his letter to Boardman's family that the government had not waited until "the first criminal" or "overt act" before stepping in. (Of course, the evidence against Burr included many acts beyond the mere expression of opinions.)

After hearing eight days' worth of argument, Chief Justice Marshall granted Burr's motion, holding that evidence of Burr's subsequent actions was inadmissible "because such testimony, being in its nature merely corroborative and incompetent to prove the overt act itself, is irrelevant until there be proof of the overt act by two witnesses." The court then ruled that no such proof had been presented: "The present indictment charges the prisoner with levying war against the United States, and alleges an overt act of levying war. That overt act must be proved, according to the mandates of the Constitution and of the act of Congress, by two witnesses. It is not proved by a single witness."[19]

This ruling—and others along the same line—may explain the jury's unusual verdict, which was delivered the following day: "We of the jury say that Aaron Burr is not proved to be guilty under this indictment by any evidence submitted to us. We therefore find him not guilty."

Burr objected to the verdict as "unusual, informal, and irregular." To some it sounded like the apocryphal verdict once rendered by a sympathetic Texas jury: "We find the man who shot his wife's lover not guilty." Chief Justice Marshall agreed to enter the formal verdict as one of "not guilty," despite the jury's unwillingness to change its particular wording.

Jefferson was outraged at the verdict. Burr had apparently won largely as a result of Marshall's interpretation of the "overt act" requirement of the Fifth Amendment's treason clause. The very concept that Jefferson believed, as expressed in his letter to Boardman, would serve as a shield against judicial restrictions on freedom of expression had been used as a sword by Aaron Burr to plot against the United States. Moreover, the sword had been unsheathed by Chief Justice John Marshall, who was a Jefferson antagonist. But that is in the nature of legal protections, such as that afforded by the "overt act" requirement. What is a shield for some becomes a sword for others—or, as Dostoyevsky put it, "A knife that cuts both ways."

What, then, does the Burr case teach us about how Jefferson might have reacted to the current threats of terrorism? Aaron Burr was not a terrorist, though his threat to the new republic may have been in some ways comparable to those posed by Islamic extremists who seek to destabilize our nation (and our world) today. Jefferson apparently believed that Burr's plans, statements, and actions constituted a real threat to the nation. He may even have believed that Burr was a threat to his own life, since—according to Justice Marshall's biographer—there was "an account of Burr's intentions to assassinate Jefferson."[20] Whether or not he exaggerated these threats—either in his own mind or publicly—he certainly overreacted to them by involving himself so deeply (and, in my view, improperly) in an ongoing judicial proceeding. The noble ends in this case (convicting and punishing a traitor who threatened our nation) justified—at least to Jefferson—some rather ignoble means: namely, crude attempts to influence the outcome of a trial. This was surely not Jefferson at his best.

Jefferson failed in his efforts to influence the outcome of the case, as he had previously failed to influence the Senate trial against Justice Samuel Chase. His failures became important building blocks of the independence of our judiciary and of the ability of judges to act as checks against the excesses of the executive. The fact that Chief Justice John Marshall may have resisted Jefferson's pressures in the Burr case because of his own strong anti-Jefferson political views simply illustrates one of the reasons why our system of checks and balances is so important in the governance of human beings who are far from angels. As James Madison wrote in *The Federalist* No. 51:

> What is government itself, but the greatest of all reflections on human nature? If men were angels, no government would be necessary. If angels were to govern men, neither external nor internal controls on government would be necessary. In framing a government which is to be administered by men over men, the great difficulty lies in this: you must first enable the government to control the governed; and in the next place oblige it to control itself. A dependence on the people is, no doubt, the primary control on the government; but experience has taught mankind the necessity of auxiliary precautions.

Jefferson himself echoed this approach to the governance of fallible human beings in his first inaugural address: "Sometimes it is said that man can not be trusted with the government of himself. Can he, then, be trusted with the government of others? Or have we found angels in the forms of kings to govern him? Let history answer this question."

History has answered this question by showing that every generation—and nearly every great president—has demonstrated human imperfections and an ability to offer justifications for believing that the particular crisis he faces warrants extraordinary measures, even if these violate the letter or the spirit of the Constitution. For Adams (supported by Washington), the threat of France justified the Alien and Sedition Acts. For Jefferson, the threat posed by Burr justified the placing of his thumb on the scale of justice. For Lincoln, the Civil War justified his suspension of the writ of habeas corpus. For Wilson, the fear of anarchism following World War I justified the Palmer Raids and the prosecution of radicals. For Roosevelt, the fear of espionage and sabotage following the attack on Pearl Harbor justified the detention of more than a hundred thousand Japanese Americans. And these were among our wisest and most humane presidents. When the Supreme Court rebuked Lincoln for his highhandedness in dealing with enemies of the Union, it warned quite presciently that the framers of our Constitution

foresaw that troublous times would arise, when rules and people would become restive under restraint, and seek by sharp and decisive measures to accomplish ends deemed just and proper; and that the principles of constitutional liberty would be in peril, unless established by irrepealable law. . . .

This nation . . . has no right to expect that it will always have wise and humane rulers, sincerely attached to the principles of the Constitution. Wicked men, ambitious of power, with hatred of liberty and contempt of law, may fill the place once occupied by

Washington and Lincoln, and if this right [to suspend provisions of the Constitution during the great exigencies of government] is conceded, and the calamities of war again befall us, the dangers to human liberty are frightful to contemplate.[21]

It is not always easy to distinguish between "wise and humane rulers sincerely attached to the principles of the Constitution," on the one hand, and "wicked men, ambitious of power, with hatred of liberty and contempt of law," on the other hand. At the time they are acting, most leaders—at least, in democracies—enjoy popular support. It is only in retrospect, and not always even then, that the distinction becomes clear. When politicians die, they are nearly always praised by other politicians. As Voltaire remarked, when informed of the death of a person he did not like, "He was a staunch patriot, a talented writer, a loyal friend, a devoted husband and father—provided he is really dead." Moreover, in practice the distinction between good and bad leaders is generally not as extreme as in the previous quoted dichotomy. Wise and humane leaders often do unwise and inhumane things, as Roosevelt did. Wise and humane leaders often show "contempt for the law," as Lincoln did.[22] When the law makes it difficult or impossible for presidents to achieve their goals with efficiency and speed, they often express contempt for the courts: as Andrew Jackson famously said of the chief justice when a ruling (*Worcester v. Georgia*, 1832) didn't go his way, "John Marshall has made his decision; now let him enforce it." Wise and humane leaders are often "ambitious of power"—that is how they became leaders! And wise and humane leaders sometimes hate liberty when that liberty is manifested by license to condemn and attack them.[23]

History has shown that it is not necessary to be a "wicked man" to do wicked things. General circumstances, in addition to personal characteristics, determine what leaders are willing to do in times of crisis. Thomas Paine famously wrote about a time that "tries men's souls." Nearly every generation of Americans has experienced circumstances that try not only the souls, but the commitment to law and liberty, of most men and women. Today we live in an age of terrorism—an age that is particularly frightening because of the invisibility of its perpetrators, the irrationality (at least to us) of their motives, and the unpredictability of their next targets. Some good men and women are prepared to do bad things to increase our security against this menace. Other good men and women are unwilling even to acknowledge that there is a menace. Wise people recognize the dangers and understand the need to eschew unrealistic absolutes and to try to strike a proper balance between liberty and security.

Jefferson understood the need to strike such balances. He also understood the need to stand strong in defense of the most basic of liberties, especially the freedom of speech, without which other liberties become impossible to defend. But he failed his own test of principle—as other great presidents before him and since have done—when the threat was close to home, as he apparently believed it was in the Burr case.

13

Jefferson's Views on Torture, Habeas Corpus, and Other Issues Currently Debated in the Context of Terrorism

Although Jefferson acted inconsistently with his own principles in the Burr case, he satisfied his own high standards with regard to several other issues currently being debated in the context of terrorism. The first is the use of torture to obtain information believed to be necessary to prevent an imminent act of mass-casualty terrorism—the so-called ticking-bomb terrorist. It may surprise you to learn that the constitutional privilege against self-incrimination, contained in the Fifth Amendment, would not prohibit the use of torture for such a *preventive* purpose, at least as it has been interpreted by the Supreme Court.

That court ruled, in 2003, that the privilege is violated *only* when the *fruits* of an interrogation employing torture are admitted against the person who was tortured, *in a criminal prosecution.* In other words, the privilege against self-incrimination, according to the Supreme Court, is nothing more than a constitutional rule of evidence that comes into play only if the tortured defendant is placed on trial. The act of introducing the fruits of the torture is prohibited. The act of torture itself, however, is not prohibited by the privilege, although it is possible—but not certain—that torture might be banned, at least in some circumstances, by the "due process" clause.

Jefferson preferred a more direct approach: he "would have replaced Mason's words on compelled self incrimination"—the words that, with some changes, became the Fifth Amendment privilege against self-incrimination—with a simple ban on the use of all torture.[1] Such an absolute ban would have been equally applicable to the use of torture for *preventive* or *self-incriminating* purposes.

Whether Jefferson would have allowed for any exceptions to this general prohibition in cases involving grave threats to multiple potential victims is, of course, impossible to know with any degree of certainty, especially in light of what he wrote about the unwritten laws of necessity and self-preservation being superior to written laws. We do know, of course, that in the Burr case, witnesses were pressured and threatened, but nothing even approaching physical torture was ever employed, despite Jefferson's apparent belief that the stakes for the new nation were quite high.

What can be inferred from Jefferson's letter to Boardman and from his preference for an across-the-board prohibition on torture is that Jefferson generally favored absolute prohibitions over balancing tests that must be administered by judges in the exercise of judicial discretion. He feared reliance on the "conscience" of judges perhaps because of the undemocratic and elitist nature of the judiciary in the abstract—lifetime appointees with no accountability to the electorate—or perhaps because of his suspicion of the particular judges he had encountered, many of whom had been appointed by his political opponents. As Jefferson wrote to John Tyler on May 26, 1810:

> We have long enough suffered under the base prostitution of law to party passions in one judge, and the imbecility of another. In the hands of one the law is nothing more than an ambiguous text, to be explained by his sophistry into any meaning which may subserve his personal malice. Nor can any milk-and-water associate maintain his own dependance, and by a firm pursuance of what the law really is, extend its protection to the citizens or the public. I believe you will do it, and where you cannot induce your colleague to do what is right, you will be firm enough to hinder him from doing what is wrong, and by opposing sense to sophistry, leave the juries free to follow their own judgment.
>
> I have long lamented with you the depreciation of law science.[2]

And later, as he mused in his autobiographical draft fragment:

> It is not enough that honest men are appointed judges. All know the influence of interest on the mind of man, and how unconsciously his judgment is warped by that influence. To this bias add that of the esprit de corps,

of their peculiar maxim and creed that "it is the office of a good judge to enlarge his jurisdiction," and the absence of responsibility, and how can we expect impartial decision between the General government, of which they are themselves so eminent a part, and an individual state from which they have nothing to hope or fear. We have seen too, that contrary to all correct example, they are in the habit of going out of the question before them, to throw an anchor ahead and grapple further hold for future advances of power. They are then in fact the corps of sappers & miners, steadily working to undermine the independant rights of the States, & to consolidate all power in the hands of that government in which they have so important a freehold estate.

By "sappers and miners," Jefferson was presumably referring to federalist judges, many of whom were appointed at the end of John Adams's presidency and who supported the power of the federal government over the "rights" of the states.[3]

Jefferson feared the power of judges to weaken the written words of the Constitution through their power of interpretation, as he wrote to Wilson Cary in 1803, "Our peculiar security is in possession of a written constitution. Let us not make it a blank paper by construction."[4]

His preference for an unambiguous prohibition on torture, over a vague evidentiary rule subject to evisceration by judges, has surely been vindicated by history. The second issue of relevance to current debates is the suspension of habeas corpus, which the Constitution specifies may be done only "when in Cases of Rebellion or Invasion the public Safety may require it." The writ of habeas corpus, known as the Great Writ, provides a mechanism for challenging all forms of detention. It requires the detaining authority to justify the detention of the subject or to release him. Jefferson believed that the Constitution was too permissive in allowing suspension of this important right. In a letter to James Madison dated July 31, 1788, in Paris, he wrote the following:

Why suspend the habeas corpus in insurrections and rebellions? The parties who may be arrested, may be charged instantly with a well-defined crime; of course, the judge will remand them. If the public safety requires that the government should have a man imprisoned on less probable testimony, in those than in other emergencies, let him be taken and tried, retaken and retried, while the necessity continues, only giving him against the government, for damages. Examine the history of England. See how few of the cases of the suspension of the habeas corpus law have been worthy of that suspension. They have been either real treason, wherein the parties might have been charged at once, or sham plots, where it was shameful they should ever have been suspected. Yet for the few cases wherein the suspension of the habeas corpus has done real good, that operation is now become habitual, and the minds of the nation almost prepared to live under its constant suspensions.[5]

He apparently trusted judges enough to insist that their power to inquire into detentions should not be abrogated, though he trusted jurors even more, characterizing them as "this sacred palladium of liberty."[6]

Jefferson's approach to the writ of habeas corpus reveals a jurisprudential philosophy that seems to run through his writings and his actions. He generally insisted on preserving important rights intact, at least in principle and in theory, while being willing to compromise them in practice by somewhat less principled actions. In the Burr case, he apparently urged his supporters in Congress to try to suspend the writ for three months, in order to put pressure on witnesses.[7] Even when he opposed formal suspension of the Great Writ, he proposed other questionable means—denying bail, arrest on less than probable cause, repeated retrials, and financial compensation for unlawful imprisonment—for accomplishing the same result. I have elsewhere referred to this approach as exploiting the "stretch points of liberty."[8]

Jefferson's conception of individual rights was complex and seems to have changed over time. When he wrote the Declaration of Independence, he characterized certain individual rights as "unalienable"—that is, not subject to being balanced against interests or powers. These rights were based on the "Laws of Nature and of Nature's God" and were endowed to all human beings by "their Creator." On the other hand, in order to secure the rights, "Governments are instituted among men, deriving their just Powers from the Consent of the Governed." In other words, abstract natural rights are not enough to govern. We also need written laws that allocate and limit powers—namely, a Constitution. In exercising these powers, the representatives of the "Governed" may sometimes alienate certain rights, thus creating a clash between pure democracy and constrained democracy. Jefferson elaborated on the nature of democracy in his first inaugural:

During the contest of opinion through which we have passed the animation of discussions and of exertions has sometimes worn an aspect which might impose on strangers unused to think freely and to speak and to write what they think; but this being now decided by the voice of the nation, announced according to the rules of the Constitution, all will, of course, arrange themselves under the will of the law, and unite in common efforts for the common good. All, too, will bear in mind this sacred principle, that though the will of the majority is in all cases to prevail, that will to be rightful must be reasonable; that the minority possess their equal rights, which equal law must protect, and to violate would be oppression.[9]

Jefferson recognized the potential conflict between "unalienable rights," on the one hand, and the democratic principle of majority rule, on the other hand. The broader and more inclusive the scope of unalienable rights, the greater the potential conflict with majority rule, since the majority will often demand results that may infringe on some unalienable rights of the minority. This will be especially true during times of crisis, and particularly so when the crisis involves a perceived conflict between the majority and a despised or feared minority, as the present terrorist crisis does, and as did many of our past crises, involving Japanese Americans, communists, radicals, Confederate sympathizers, and "Jacobins."

If the will of the majority prevails, then the unalienable rights of some minorities will sometimes be alienated. If minority rights prevail, then the will of the majority will often be thwarted. The conflict was particularly daunting for Jefferson, since under our Constitution—at least, as interpreted by John Marshall—it was the role of the judiciary to resolve this conflict in particular cases and controversies, and Jefferson simply didn't trust judges to enforce the unalienable rights of minorities. He trusted juries, voters, and elected representatives more than he did lifetime-appointed judges to protect minorities. The verdict of history has not acquitted this trust in the people. Nor has it necessarily acquitted—at least in the long run—the trust placed by many current civil libertarians in the judiciary.[10] The best assurance that rights will be appreciated and enforced is if they become part of the broad-based cultural consensus to which every branch of government is expected to be sensitive.

The Declaration speaks about rights in more absolute terms than the Constitution does. That is quite understandable since the Declaration is essentially a lawless document. Separation from England was an act of revolution—of treason. It could not be based on the governing positive law, which was, of course, English. It had to invoke a *higher* law—the law of nature and of nature's God. The higher the law, the more abstract and absolute it is likely to be.

The Constitution, on the other hand, is a practical prescription for governance under law. It is a conservative document written by those in power and designed not for revolution but for maintenance of the status quo. Constitutions are inevitably more conservative than are calls to arms. Hannah Arendt may have overstated this phenomenon when she wrote, "[T]he most radical revolutionary will become a conservative the day after the revolution,"[11] but she certainly makes an important point. Although Jefferson never quite abandoned his revolutionary zeal—he famously wrote in 1787 that "the tree of liberty must be refreshed from time to time with the blood of patriots and tyrants"[12]—he handed over the task of Constitution writing to his more cautious protégé James Madison. The resulting Constitution does not invoke God—either nature's or the Bible's. Nor does it mention natural law. It is largely a mechanistic blueprint for governance with checks and balances, separation of power, and federalism. It seeks to balance rights and interests. Its amending process is cumbersome and difficult. Even the Bill of Rights—appended four years after the Constitution was ratified—speaks in the language of constraints on governmental power, rather than in the language of absolute and unalienable rights. The First Amendment, for example, does not convey an absolute right to freedom of expression. Rather, it precludes *Congress* from making any law abridging the freedom of speech.

As Jefferson wrote to Abigail Adams, "While we deny that Congress have a right to controul the freedom of the press, we have ever asserted the right of the states, and their exclusive right, to do so. They have accordingly, all of them, made provisions for punishing slander, which those who have time and inclination resort to for the vindication of their characters."[13]

The First Amendment has now been held applicable to the states through the Fourteenth Amendment, but even so, it does not confer on individuals any absolute right of free speech. As I once explained in a *New York Times* op-ed dealing with the power of Major League Baseball to suspend John Rocker, who had expressed bigoted views:

> Despite the common myth that we can say anything we please in this country, the fact is that our Bill of Rights does not grant Americans any general right of free speech.
>
> The First Amendment prohibits "Congress," and by modern interpretation, federal and state governments from "abridging the freedom of speech, or of the press." The amendment, then, is a restriction on

government power, not a right to say anything without fear of all consequences. The First Amendment says nothing about the power of private employers, universities, or sports leagues to censor or punish speakers who express views with which they disagree.

Thus, [Bud] Selig was well within his rights as the chief executive of a private corporation to make an independent decision to suspend Rocker.

I went on to argue, however, that Selig's decision

violates the *spirit* of free speech that animates the First Amendment [and, may I add, Jefferson's views on freedom of speech as reflected in his letter to Boardman]. The Constitution may impose limits only on the government, but the First Amendment is premised on the idea that there should be a free marketplace of ideas. Private universities, for example, are not constrained by the Constitution, but most choose to follow it anyway, because they recognize that the exchange of ideas—no matter how wrongheaded or obnoxious—is good for education. . . .

Baseball is not, of course, a university, and diversity of views is not essential to the enterprise. But trash talking, banter, razzing, and taunting have always been part of the game. However offensive his comments, Rocker had every right to insult New York and New Yorkers. He crossed the line when he moved to racist and ethnic stereotyping, but he is surely not the first player to have expressed such views. Will baseball now need a platoon of speech cops monitoring players in bars and at barbeques? Or will the new rule be limited to published comments? What about taunts on the field?

Now that baseball has drawn a line in the sand, it must apply it uniformly.

Selig would have been wiser not to suspend Rocker, but to announce that the league is committed to freedom of speech and that the comments of individual players should not be misunderstood as reflecting the opinions of major-league baseball.[14]

Other rights enumerated in the Bill of Rights are also not absolute. The Fourth Amendment protects against "unreasonable" searches, as the Eighth Amendment prohibits "unreasonable" bail. Other amendments have been interpreted over the years in a nuanced and calibrated manner.[15]

Practical governance—as distinguished from revolution—is not feasible in the face of absolute and unalienable rights. All governments throughout time and place have alienated rights, especially during times of crisis. Even during normal times, rights are balanced against other rights, interests, and powers. That is the reality of governance, though the rhetoric often disguises it.

But rhetoric, too, has a role to play in governance. It may be useful to *assert* that some rights are absolute and unalienable. This is a *tactic* employed by some in an effort to assure that when the balance is ultimately struck—as they know it must be—it will be struck in favor of those rights when they come into inevitable conflict with other considerations. This tactic was employed by Jefferson in his draft of the Declaration and, to a somewhat lesser degree, in his subsequent writings.

The opposite approach is to acknowledge candidly that rights must always be subjected to a balancing approach, and that the balance should generally be struck in favor of rights, but that there may be extreme circumstances under which rights must be compromised or alienated in the interest of security. Benjamin Franklin famously declared that "they who can give up essential liberty to obtain a little temporary safety deserve neither liberty nor safety." The operative words are *essential liberty* and *little temporary safety*. Not all rights are as essential as others, and sometimes what is at stake is more than a "little temporary safety." This, surely, is the situation with regard to incitement by radical imams of mass-casualty suicide terrorism.

14

——⪼●⪻——

How Would Jefferson Strike the Balance between Freedom of Speech and Prevention of Terrorism?

The situation we confront today, and the one on which I wish we could secure the benefit of Jefferson's wisdom, is far too complicated to be resolved by Benjamin Franklin's pithy aphorism. When radical imams preach violence and encourage suicide terrorism, the considerations at stake on both sides are among the most "essential" to any democracy. On one side are the rights to freedom of expression, freedom of religion, and freedom of association. These rights are central to the workings of democracy, and they should not be compromised or alienated except under the most extreme circumstances, and even then in the most circumscribed and temporary manner. As Jefferson once put it:

181

"[T]he liberty of speaking and writing guards our other liberties." On the other side are the dangers posed by mass-victim suicide terrorism—dangers that threaten not only our security but democracy itself. What is at stake in balancing freedom of expression against prevention of terrorism is neither inessential liberties nor "a little temporary safety," but rather the most essential of liberties, the most basic safety, and the survival of open, pluralistic democracy. How to strike the appropriate balances in this context is the testing conflict of our generation.

There are essentially three ways to address this issue. The first is to be completely open and candid. This requires an express acknowledgment that the right of the imams to preach violence and the right of their audiences to listen to their dangerous sermons must be balanced against the right of their potential victims to be protected against the threat of terrorism. In some extreme instances, therefore, the right of free speech will inevitably be compromised. This was the approach proposed by Reverend Stanley Griswold in his sermon.

The second approach is to declare that freedom of speech will never be compromised but then to explain that freedom of speech does not include incitements to violence. Under this approach, the right remains unalienable, but its definition, and the exceptions to it, become malleable. This was the approach employed by Justice Hugo Black on the United States Supreme Court during the 1950s and 1960s. An exchange—perhaps apocryphal—between Black and Felix Frankfurter during a Supreme Court argument in a First Amendment case involving efforts by a state to censor aptly summarizes their different positions. Black took out a copy of the Constitution and read the First Amendment to the lawyer who was arguing for censorship. Banging on the desk, Black screamed, "Congress shall make *no law—no law—no law.*" Frankfurter then got out his copy of the Constitution and read the same amendment. "*Congress—Congress—Congress* shall make no law," he shouted. Jefferson would probably have agreed with both justices since he regarded the First Amendment as containing an absolute prohibition against *the federal government* making *any* law abridging the freedom of speech. Jefferson, you will recall, would have allowed the states to punish some genres of speech that were out of bounds for the federal government. He understood that there may be "extreme cases" in which "the unwritten laws of necessity, of self-preservation, and of the public safety control the written laws." He also acknowledged that "the line of discrimination . . . may be difficult."[1]

The third approach is simply to allow the imams to continue to preach their hatred and to accept the potential consequences, even if they include mass-casualty terrorism. This is what Jefferson suggested in his letter to Boardman as his personal, as distinguished from his constitutional, opinion, but it was expressly premised on his confidence that violence could be prevented by the open marketplace of ideas and the power of the state to step in at the point of the first overt act. What if this confidence had been shattered by experience? What if Jefferson had seen with his own eyes that a libertarian approach to dangerous speech in fact led to massive violence? That the marketplace did not work? That waiting for the first criminal act resulted in mass casualties rather than safety?

Recall that Jefferson derived his philosophy from observation, experience, and reason, not from any a priori principle based on holy books or messages from God. As he wrote in 1815, "[A]ll theory must yield to experience."[2] To him, the laws of nature could be discerned by observing human beings in action. He expounded on his view of the moral sense in a letter to his nephew Peter Carr in 1787:

> The moral sense, or conscience, is as much a part of man as his leg or arm. It is given to all human beings in a stronger or weaker degree, as force of members is given them in a greater or less degree. It may be strengthened by exercise, as may any particular limb of the body. This sense is submitted indeed in some degree to the guidance of reason; but it is a small stock which is required for this: even a less one than what we call Common sense. State a moral case to a ploughman & a professor. The former will decide it as well, & often better than the latter, because he has not been led astray by rules.[3]

The moral sense of the plowman will often be "better" than that of the professor because "a little experience is worth a great deal of reading."[4]

Jefferson often changed his mind based on what he observed, and he hoped that future observations would lead him to future revisions.[5] He was the poster child for open-mindedness.

If experience led him to reject the third approach, the one espoused in his letter to Boardman—namely, to let the imams preach regardless of the feared consequences—for which of the first two would he have opted? Would he prefer an explicit limit on freedom of speech? Or an implicit redefinition of such freedom, while continuing to proclaim the absolute inalienability of the right of free speech?

Given these two options, I know what I would prefer. I always opt for explicitness and candor because I believe these qualities are essential to accountability and that accountability is essential to democracy.[6] I think Jefferson might have come out the other way—insisting that the right to absolute freedom of speech be preserved explicitly, but that the definition and scope of the right could be alienated implicitly. For Jefferson, the rhetoric of inalienability must be preserved even in the face of the pragmatic need to compromise.

There is, of course, the possibility that Jefferson would have stuck to his principles—and the views he expressed in his letter to Boardman—and simply opted to do nothing to interfere with imams who advocate and inspire violence, even if the "first criminal act produced by the false reasoning" were to be a deadly act of mass-casualty terrorism. Jefferson understood that the cost of protecting liberty—not only in dollars but in lives—could be very high. As he wrote to Ezra Stiles in 1786, "I prefer dangerous liberty to quiet servitude."[7] He and his fellow signers of the Declaration of Independence were prepared, after all, to place at risk "our lives, our fortunes, and our sacred honor," in order to secure liberty. Should we be asked to risk less to preserve the liberty with which they endowed us?

Jefferson regarded freedom of speech as part of a great experiment. He described the experiment in his second inaugural address in 1805:

Nor was it uninteresting to the world, that an experiment should be fairly and fully made, whether freedom of discussion, unaided by power, is not sufficient for the propagation and protection of truth—whether a government, conducting itself in the true spirit of its constitution, with zeal and purity, and doing no act which it would be unwilling the whole world should witness, can be written down by falsehood and defamation. The

experiment has been tried; you have witnessed the
scene; our fellow-citizens looked on, cool and collected; they saw the latent source from which these out-
rages proceeded; they gathered around their public
functionaries, and when the Constitution called them
to the decision by suffrage, they pronounced their verdict, honorable to those who had served them and con-
solatory to the friend of man who believes that he may
be trusted with the control of his own affairs.

He also regarded the states—which were free, in his view,
to try different approaches—as part of that experiment:

No inference is here intended, that the laws, provided
by the State against false and defamatory publications,
should not be enforced; he who has time, renders a
service to public morals and public tranquility, in
reforming these abuses by the salutary coercions of the
law; but the experiment is noted, to prove that, since
truth and reason have maintained their ground against
false opinions in league with false facts, the press,
confined to truth, needs no other legal restraint; the
public judgment will correct false reasonings and opinions, on a full hearing of all parties; and no other defi-
nite line can be drawn between the inestimable liberty
of the press and its demoralizing licentiousness. If
there be still improprieties which this rule would not
restrain, its supplement must be sought in the censorship of public opinion.

Today, the states have no more power to regulate speech
than does the federal government. Both the states and the
federal government are equally bound by the prohibition of

the First Amendment against making any law abridging the freedom of speech, press, religion, free exercise, or assembly. Nor is the "censorship of public opinion" available to counter the threat posed by imams who preach violence in the privacy of their insular mosques. The freedom of imams to preach such violence is indeed a "dangerous liberty." There is no easy or risk-free option. We must choose between the real risks of terrorism and the equally real risks of censorship.

15

My View, as Influenced
by Jefferson and the
Experiences of Our Time

I end this book with my own opinion regarding the
issue raised by the Griswold-Boardman-Jefferson
exchange. My opinion is influenced equally by those who
came before me—most particularly, Jefferson—and that
which I have experienced in my many years of involvement
in the struggle both to preserve the right to uncensored
speech and to act effectively but reasonably against the real
dangers of terrorism. Having weighed all the opinions, I
would follow the course laid out in Jefferson's letter to
Boardman, but without the confidence he expressed in the
safety of that course.

I would not censor the imams' expression of immoral and dangerous views. I would wait for the "first crimes" produced "by [their] false reasoning." I would not authorize the law to treat "the utterance of an opinion"—or even the advocacy of a course of conduct—as "an overt act." But I do not share Jefferson's opinion that we can pursue this course "safely" and that we have "nothing to fear from" the potential consequences. We have much to fear and we should take all reasonable steps, consistent with preserving our liberties, to prevent further acts of terrorism.

We also would have much to fear from restricting the free speech of dangerous and immoral imams because experience shows that the appetite of the censor, once stimulated, is rarely sated. There is a concept in Jewish tradition that one sin promotes other sins and one good deed promotes other good deeds.[1] The same may be true of both censorship and freedom of speech. Each is a slippery slope, and it is safer—though not entirely safe—to slide down the slope of more speech than down the slope of more censorship.

The decision whether to endure dangerous speech or to censor can never be made with absolute certainty about the consequences. It always involves probabilistic assessments and untrustworthy predictions. It is never certain that a given speech or genre of speech will produce violent actions. Nor can it be certain that it won't. There will always be doubt, and the law's most daunting task is to articulate rules for how to decide complex issues in the face of inevitable doubt.

Human conduct is determined by multiple factors. Terrorism is a product of numerous pressures. A particularly provocative speech by a particularly charismatic preacher may serve as a trigger, but the gun must already be loaded. The "loaded" terrorist may, however, be provoked by something other than a speech—perhaps by a news event, a family crisis, a psychological breakdown. There is rarely a direct one-to-one causal relationship between a particular speech and an act of violence, despite Reverend Stanley Griswold's suggestion to the contrary in his sermon.[2]

In addition, censorship or punishment of a speaker is not always effective in preventing violence. It would be difficult to craft a narrow rule that would be effective against dangerous imams but that would not also cover "good" speech that should be constitutionally protected. When I was criticized for opposing the censorship efforts of Skokie, Illinois, against the neo-Nazis, I issued a challenge to my critics: draft a constitutional law that could be applied against the neo-Nazis marching through Skokie that couldn't also be applied against Martin Luther King marching through Birmingham. No one came up with such a law. The same challenge could be made with regard to a law applicable to imams that would not be applicable to ministers railing against abortion, homosexuality, racial injustice, or war. Censorship laws are blunt instruments, not sharp scalpels. Once enacted, they are easily misapplied to merely unpopular or only marginally dangerous speech. Under our First Amendment, a censorship law would have to be written in broad general language and could not be directed at specific religious, ethnic, racial, or political groups. Any such law could be misused by politicians to censor their political enemies or other "undesirable" groups.

Moreover, censorship laws—at least those that could pass muster under our Constitution—could easily be evaded by clever imams. A law punishing direct incitement could be circumvented by vague, poetic, or symbolic advocacy of "justice." We have seen examples of such preaching in England, France, Gaza, and the West Bank. Coded messages are difficult for the uninitiated to decipher but send a clear message to those who already agree with the messenger.

For all these reasons and more, the potential speculative benefits of censorship, in terms of terrorist prevention, would appear to be outweighed by the potential costs of any censorship rule—at least under the current circumstances.

In the spirit of Jefferson, however, we should always keep an open mind even about the most basic of rights. I hope we will never see a time when the threat of terrorism pushes us toward censorship—even of those who would destroy all of our rights in the name of their "false reasoning" and "evident" immorality.

In a letter written to Judge John Tyler—whose son would become our tenth president—Thomas Jefferson mused about his legacy to his "successors."

No experiment can be more interesting than that we are now trying, and which we trust will end in establishing the fact that man may be governed by reason and truth. Our first object should therefore be, to leave open to him all the avenues to truth. The most effectual hitherto found, is the freedom of the press. It is, therefore, the first step up by those who fear the investigation of their actions. The firmness with which the people have withstood the late abuses of the press, the discernment they have manifested between truth and falsehood show that they may safely be trusted to hear everything true and false, and to form a correct judgment between them. As little is it necessary to impose on their senses, or dazzle their minds by pomp splendor, or forms. Instead of this artificial how much surer is the real respect, which results from the use of their reason, and the habit of bringing everything to the test of common sense.

I hold it, therefore, certain, that to open the doors of truth, and to fortify the habit of testing everything by reason, are the most effectual manacles we can rivet on the hands of [our] successors to prevent their manacling the people with their own consent.[3]

Under these criteria—"common sense," "reason," "trusting," and "truth"—the "safer" course is to "leave open" to everyone "all the avenues to truth," instead of trusting "the conscience of the judge" to serve as the traffic cop of ideas.

We are Jefferson's successors, and we are still part of the great "experiment" on which he and his generation of founders embarked. All experiments are dangerous. None are completely predictable. Let us continue in the risky but rewarding direction toward which Jefferson pointed us, two centuries ago, in the hope that "the doors of truth" will long remain wide open for us and our successors. Let us hope that Jefferson's admonition to Reverend Griswold to trust the "good sense" of his fellow citizens and "go the whole length of sound principle" by rejecting the seductive lure of the censor will remain the American way even in the face of bloody terrorism. Thomas Jefferson's letter of July 3, 1801, to Elijah Boardman remains as relevant today as it was when it was written more than two centuries ago. I cherish having this Jefferson letter in my collection and being able to publish it and place it in context for all to read.

APPENDIX A

A Transcript of the Jefferson Letter and a Letterpress Copy

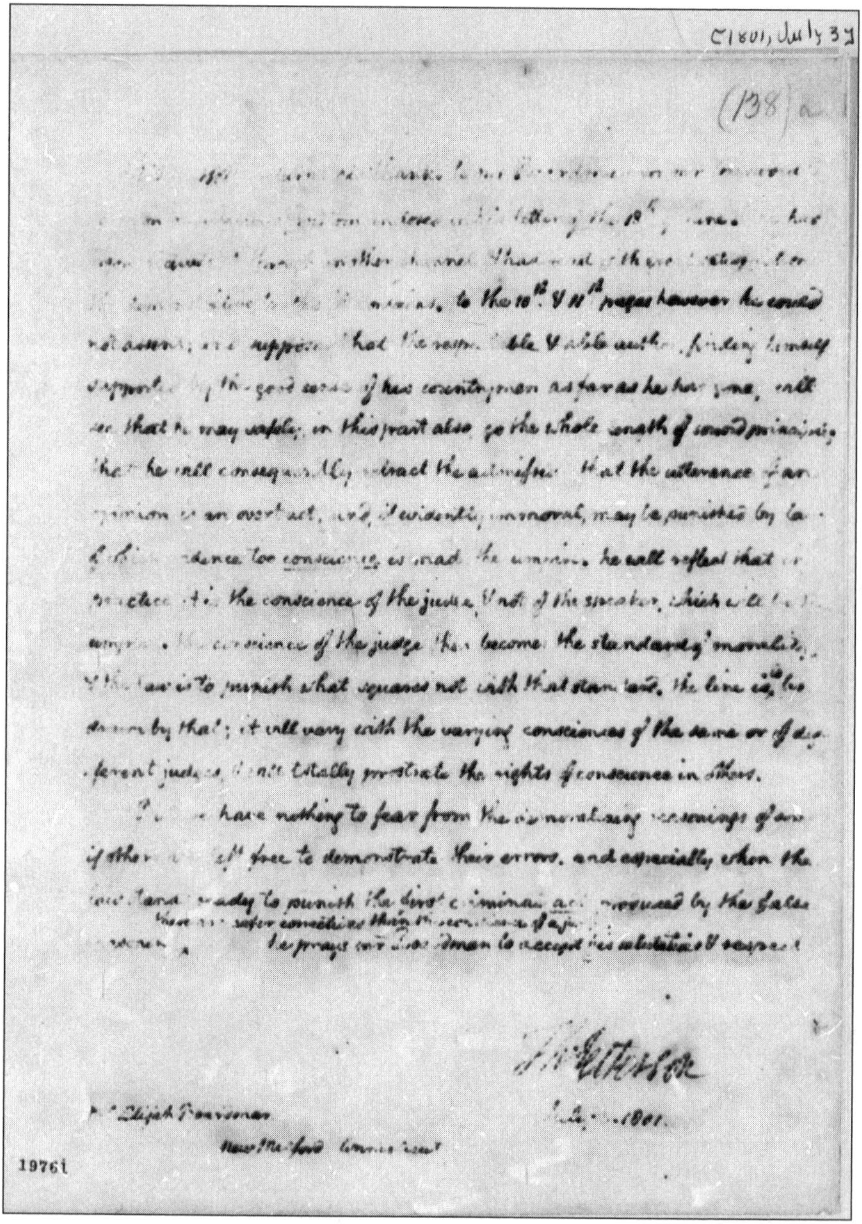

[1801, July 3]

(138)

[illegible]

[illegible] to the 10th & 11th pages however he could not assent; & he supposes that the respectable & able author, finding himself supported by the good sense of his countrymen as far as he has gone, will see that he may safely, in this part also, go the whole length of sound principle; that he will consequently retract the admission that the utterance of an opinion is an overt act, and, if evidently immoral, may be punished by law. if [illegible] dence too conscience is made the umpire, he will reflect that in practice it is the conscience of the judge, & not of the speaker, which will be the umpire. the conscience of the judge then becomes the standard of morality, & the law is to punish what squares not with that standard, the line is to be drawn by that; it will vary with the varying consciences of the same or of different judges, & will totally prostrate the rights of conscience in others.

[illegible] have nothing to fear from the demoralising reasonings of some if others are left free to demonstrate their errors. and especially when the law stands ready to punish the first criminal act produced by the false reasoning; there are safer correctives than the conscience of a judge. he prays Mr. Boardman to accept his salutations & respect.

Th: Jefferson

Mr. Elijah Boardman July 3. 1801.

New Milford Connecticut

19761

Letterpress Version of Jefferson's Letter

Th Jefferson returns his thanks to Mr. Boardman for Mr. Griswold's sermon on religious freedom, inclosed in his letter of the 18th of June. he had before received it through another channel, & had read with great satisfaction the demonstrative truths it contains. to the 10th and 11th pages however he count not assent; and supposes that the respectable & able author, finding himself supported by the good sense of his countrymen as far as he has gone, will see that he may safely, in this part also, go the whole length of sound principle that he will consequently retract the admission that the utterance of an opinion is an overt act, and if evidently immoral may be punished by law of which evidence too *conscience* is made the umpire. he will reflect that in practice it is the conscience of the judge, & not of the speaker, which will be the umpire. the conscience of judge then becomes the standard of morality &* the law is to punish what squares not with that standard. the line is to be drawn by that; it will vary with the varying consciences of the same or of different judges & will totally prostrate the rights of conscience in others.

But we have nothing to fear from the demoralizing reasonings of some, if others are left free to demonstrate their errors. and especially the law stands ready to punish the first criminal act produced by false reasoning. these are safer correctives than the conscience of a judge. he prays Mr. Boardman to accept his salutations and respect.

Th[?] Jefferson

The word is either "&" or "if." The context supports either, and the shape of the letters is consistent with both. I believe it is more likely an ampersand.

APPENDIX B

Excerpted from "Discourse: Truth Its Own Test and God Its Only Judge"

A Sermon Delivered by Stanley Griswold,
October 12, 1800

Copy of the sermon obtained from the American Antiquarian Society in
Worcester, Massachusetts.

TRUTH ITS OWN TEST AND GOD ITS
ONLY JUDGE.

OR,

AN INQUIRY,—HOW FAR MEN MAY CLAIM
AUTHORITY OVER EACH OTHER'S
RELIGIOUS OPINIONS?

A

DISCOURSE,

DELIVERED AT

NEW-MILFORD,

OCTOBER 12th, 1800.

By STANLEY GRISWOLD,
Pastor of a Church in New-Milford.

" *Magna est veritas et prevælebit.*"
" *The truth shall make you free.*"

BRIDGEPORT: [Conn.]
PRINTED BY LAZARUS BEACH.
—1800—

200

How far men may set up authority over each other's opinions? Or, how far each individual has a right to enjoy his own thoughts without molestation, pain or penalty, in good name, prosperity, life or any thing whatever, from his fellow creatures. . . .

I purpose to take up the subject on a very general scale, and give it as critical and candid an examination as so broad a scale and my abilities will allow.

We shall first inquire, whether there is any reason that our religious opinions should be subject to the control of man or any tribunal on earth, so as to warrant the judging, 'speaking evil of,' or in any shape molesting one another on their account?

Secondly, To what man, or to what tribunal on earth, is such authority delegated by heaven? . . .

RELIGION IS A CONCERN BETWEEN THE SOUL OF A MAN AND HIS MAKER. There is something so sublime and awful in this idea, that it should seem sufficient to repress the temerity of a vain mortal who would intermeddle in this high concern. . . .

But even granting such authority were delegated, still it must be obvious to the least reaction that it could not reach to *every* case of difference in opinion. For, what two persons think exactly alike in every thing? I presume to say, two such persons never were found in this world. The minds of men differ as much as their faces. . . . Therefore, their conclusions respecting many things must be different, and as we see actually are different. In order to have two persons think precisely alike about every thing, they must see through the same eyes, have the same temptations, interests and passions, . . . in a word, must be exact duplicates of each other; which never was, and probable never will be the case.

If then the minds of no two can be thoroughly and precisely alike, it follows, either that the world must be constantly full of complaints, processes, trials, condemnations, mutual censures and molestations, each one hauling and being hauled in his turn before tribunals; or else, that this business of judging and molesting must not extend to *all* cases of difference in opinion.

The former I believe has struck every one, who has thought of it, with abhorrence, that we all should be constantly impeaching, condemning, censuring, endeavoring to subject one another to privations, disabilities, penalties, every day and every moment, for every thing wherein we differ in opinion! It is seen, this will not do. Indeed upon this principle no such thing as society could exist. In order for society to exist, its members must "agree to differ" in some things.

Hence the necessity of a *line* being drawn somewhere among opinions to divide those which are censurable and punishable from those which are not: I mean, in case any opinions may be punished at all. What this line should be, where it should run, what it should include and what exclude, has greatly exercised the ingenuity of those who have not been willing to give up entirely their claim to authority over opinions.

Some have drawn it between those things which they call *essential* for salvation and those they call *non-essential*: or which is about the same thing, the *fundamentals* of religion and the *circumstantials*. Every one must see how this leaves the line about as obscure and precarious as if it were not attempted to be drawn at all. . . . So all is uncertainty, and no one knows on what to depend.

Others have made the line to rest of *construction, implication* or *inference:* that is, all opinions are punishable which in *their* view, or by *their construction*, lead to immorality or to the denial of some of the essentials of religion, or to some other bad consequence. . . .

When we consider this scheme of construction and inference, we see in it still more difficulties, more absurdities and more mischiefs. By this, a most unbounded scope is given to construe any thing and every thing into bad tendencies and bad consequences, even the most trivial things, . . . as much, or perhaps more, than if no rule at all were pretended.

Constructive heresy, like *constructive treason*, has produced a world of mischief. It has drawn guilt out of the purest innocence. It has charged the blackest intentions upon the best of men; has loaded the most heavenly doctrines with infernal calumny. It has turned the truth itself into lies and blasphemy. . . .

From a view of these deplorable evils which have happened by means of men's undertaking to meddle with one another for opinions, the friends of human happiness have been induced to inquire more strictly the subject of this important line; and from a fair view of scripture as well as from the dictates of humanity and philosophy, have generally come to the conclusion, that this line should be drawn entirely *around all matters of opinion*, excluding the *whole*, as being what in no case ought to subject a man to molestation from his fellow creatures. This is the ground taken by those who are for perfectly *free toleration* of religion.

This may need some explanation; but with proper explanation it appears to me every person of cool, dispassionate thought must give it his hearty concurrence. Permit me to therefore explain:

By opinion is meant *opinion merely*, and not the making use of it purposely to stir up broils and strife, wantonly to excite parties and needless divisions, or to influence others to do evil. *Opinion* strictly speaking, is what lies *within* the mind, it is our *thought* or *belief*. Divulging this opinion is an *action*, and an action for which, if it be done with the design just mentioned, a man may be accountable to society.

But, merely for *having the opinion*, for *thinking*, be the opinion what it may, even it be erroneous, I apprehend no good reason can be assigned, why a person ought to be molested by his fellow-creatures. The supposition is, he takes no pains to divulge and spread it with the sinister view to raise reactions, excite needless divisions, or to influence others to do evil. . . . In short, he wishes not to trouble or hurt his fellow creatures with it, nor does he trouble or hurt them with it. Why then should they hurt him? What ground of action have they against him? He has done no *hurt*. . . . It is strange how the usurpers of authority over men's principles, whether political or religious, have totally mistaken their own policy. For, by rigorous measures they have done more to publish and propagate the obnoxious principles, than the supporters of such principles could have done by the most perfect freedom. . . .

The position therefore is doubtless true with respect to what is strictly *opinion*, that a man ought not to be molested in any shape for his opinions, be they what they may. But, the divulging of an opinion with the wanton view to excite broils and cause needless dissentions, or to influence others to do evil, is quite a different thing. This is an *overt act*, and, as the case may be, an evident *immorality*. Yet this, I believe is often confounded in the question, how far men are liable for their opinions? And tends not a little to embarrass the subject of *free toleration*.

But I beg not to be understood as if the promulging of an opinion with an *honest view* were blameable and immoral. A person may be honest in divulging *some kinds* of opinions, believing them to be highly important to be known and embraced by mankind. In this he is no schismatic; he does it not from the wanton desire to embroil society and throw it into divisions and confusion[:] but is serious and sincere, like the apostles of old. No more than the apostles ought such an one to be molested.

But *certain opinions* may be attempted to be propagated; in which no *honest view* can possibly exist, and for which a person would justly be accountable to [illegible]. To know what these are, brings up once more the necessity of a *line*.

What then is the line which should divide those opinions which may be promulgated with impunity, from those which cannot be propagated without guilt?

This line I hold to be very plain, even so plain that "he who runs may read it". I believe there is such a thing as a *Con-*

science in man, an inherent sense of right and wrong in every intelligent creature through the world. Some speculatists have pretended to doubt the reality of such a principal in man; but were never able to divest themselves of it. . . .

We all feel this principle operating with a sure and uncontrollable sway within us. It is indeed a Monitor the Vice-gerent of God almighty in the soul. I suppose it to be inseparable from rational faculties. When we do good, it approves and speaks peace to the mind. When we do evil, it condemns and torments.

This, then, is the *line* I would have to divide between opinions, to separate those the teaching of which shall be punishable, from those which may be taught with impunity. On the one side are all those things concerning which conscience dictates something. On the other all those things concerning which she dictates nothing.

If a person should endeavor to propagate an opinion, that it is right to steal, to lie, to cheat, to rob, to murder, or to do any thing which conscience, or "the law written on the heart," plainly condemns, such person, even though he himself be not guilty of these crimes in an overt form, yet justly subjects himself to the reprehension and censure of all his fellow-creatures, and as the case may be I believe to some severer punishment. Could we be content to have a person of this description run about and inculcate these crimes upon our children and upon simple ones? Certainly we could not and ought not. Such an one ought to be taken up, and if he will not cease to teach these things, he should not only be censured and reprimanded, but absolutely confined from running at large to poison society and unhinge it from its foundations. Such an one I believe would be liable upon good principles of law and reason to be punished as an *accessory*, at least as an *advisor and mover* of the crimes of his pupil. Suppose one of his simple disciples should commit murder, and it should appear that he did it in consequence of what this person had taught him on the subject; although perhaps it should not be sufficient to hang the teacher, yet it ought to subject him to some kind of punishment, and I think of considerable severity.

But as to things concerning which conscience declares nothing, which rest entirely on exterior proof, or the mere induction of reasoning, or perhaps on nothing better than fancy or traditional prejudice, why should a person be molested on account of such things? He ought, to be sure to be compelled to use decency, fairness and civility towards others in propagating his belief, the same indeed which I am contending others should use towards him. But if he use these, (which a person honest in his opinions will always use) why should he be impeded or molested? And why should we be unwilling to hear what he has to offer in support of his belief? Why set ourselves up as infallible standards? God has written nothing on our hearts whereby we may decide as to these matters. . . . Is there nothing to be known beyond what we know, and nothing true but just as we hold it? Perhaps others have proofs which it can do us no hurt to hear. Or if we have better than they, then we ought to be allowed to offer them. This right is reciprocal, and ought ever to be held sacred. . . .

So every person should be dismissed who is brought up for advancing opinions which enter not into the nature of morals and concerning which conscience dictates nothing. But if you find a person teaching and propagating that it is right to steal your property, rob, murder you, there could not be a moments hesitation, you would know that even his own conscience condemns him, as well as yours, and the conscience of all beings in heaven and on earth, yea, and in hell. Therefore you might instantly judge, and be perfectly secure in so doing. For, here you would risqué no danger of acting against the truth, the error being apparent without the possibility of a doubt. . . . Whereas if you venture beyond the line of these matters of natural right and wrong, to scatter your censures and punishments on men and opinions of the other description, you expose yourself to the awful hazard of persecuting the truth, wounding innocence, violating honesty, injuring the best of [men], and offending your God.

The line I have pointed out I think must be clear and plain to every one. There is no mistaking it. Every creature who knows right from wrong can tell where it runs, what lies on the one side, and what on the other. . . .

Against what has been offered I am sensible some objections have been raised, and some reasons attempted to be shewn, why the opinions of men should be controlled beyond the line we have assigned. I shall not undertake to enumerate them all, but to touch upon one or two of the most plausible.

It has been said, that *we who know the truth* ought to bear down all opposition before it, and not suffer its enemies to enjoy quiet, friendship, or favor until they embrace it. Now this was the argument which excited so many in ancient times by persecution and bloodshed to "do God service." This excited the Crusaders to go against the Mahometans. . . . But permit me to correct that expression, that "*we who know the truth* should bear down all opposition before it." It is not *we* that should bear down the opposition: it is the *Truth* that should bear it down. And let Truth stand upon her own basis, clothed only with her own charms, and there is no danger but that in due time all opposition would be borne down and cease. In the mean time, it is *our* duty to treat our brethren of other sentiments with civility and a becoming deference, troubling them only with arguments, love, and kindness.

But, it has been said, it is necessary for the purpose of *civil government*, or the *good of the state*, that the people should be of one mind, one religion. As this is what lies very much at the bottom of all religious compulsion and of all the opposition to the doctrine I contend for, it will be considered at some length.

On the very ground that it is desirable, and would be useful for the state, that the people should be of one religion, I dispute the propriety of *compelling* them to be so. For, I believe the best, and indeed the only way to bring people to be of one mind is to suffer them to think freely for themselves. The Christian world has for a long time been trying, by test-laws and persecution of heretics, to prevent schism, to preserve their people in one mind, or bring back those who have strayed, to the unity of the faith. But they have totally mistaken the *means*; and America bids fair to be the first to teach them what those means are. The means to do this, are so far from compulsion or the least manner of violence, that they are the very opposite. The interests of men are about the same both for this world and another. And intelligence is the same faculty in all. Why then should they not come to nearly the same conclusions on all important subjects, which have any interests of moment in them and which admit arguments of weight to be used, provided they might pursue freely their inquiries? Either men are *reasonable* beings, or they are *not*. If reasonable, then the faculty which distinguishes them as a race will lead them to similar conclusions from similar premises. If they are not reasonable beings, then fence them, fetter them, beat, drive them, as you do your brutes; for, no more than brutes are they capable of any religion which derives the name, nor is it any matter what they believe. But I hold that men are a race of rational beings. . . . Let them then be treated as such. . . .

If *reason* were a variable thing[,] or if *truth* were a variable thing, in either case I could not be so confidant of the justice of these remarks. But if any thing be meant by *rational faculties* above the mere passion of brutes, I think they must be uniform, in all who possess them, directing men to similar ends, as instinct directs the brutes to similar ends. . . .

Or if any thing be meant by truth, that is truth, and not whatever you please to make it, then to a free mind it must appear; and it must appear powerful and commanding.

NOTES

1 My Passion for Collecting

1. James O. Freedman, *Finding the Words: The Education of James O. Freedman* (Princeton, NJ: Princeton University Press, 2007), p. 122.
2. Ibid., p. 130.
3. Ibid., p. 134.

2 My Passions for Freedom of Speech, Criminal Law, and Thomas Jefferson

1. Lewis Carroll, *The Annotated Alice* (New York: W. W. Norton, 2000), pp. 196–198.
2. The article is included in my book *Shouting Fire* (Boston: Little, Brown, 2002), pp. 142–147.
3. Josh Gerstein, "Gingrich: Free Speech Should Be Curtailed to Fight Terrorism," *New York Sun*, November 29, 2006, p. 4.
4. See www.publications.parliament.uk/pa/cm200506/cmbills/011/2006011.pdf, for the text of the original bill. See www.opsi.gov.uk/ACTS/acts2006/ukpga_20060001_en.pdf, accessed May 1, 2007, for the final text of the bill, and Rushdie's "A Small Victory for Freedom of Speech in U.K.," *Toronto Star*, February 14, 2006, p. A17.
5. See Alan Dershowitz, *The Best Defense* (New York: Random House, 1982), p. 4.
6. See Alan Dershowitz, *Why Terrorism Works: Understanding the Threat, Responding to the Challenge* (New Haven, CT: Yale University Press, 2002), p. 113. Citing "Eskin Gets Four Months for Curse on Rabin," *Jerusalem Post*, July 21, 1997.
7. Dershowitz, *Why Terrorism Works*, p. 222.

8. Alan Dershowitz, "The Greatest Threat to Civil Liberties Would Be Another Atrocity Like 9/11," *Spectator*, September 2, 2006.
9. Mardy Grothe, *Oxymoronica: Paradoxical Wit and Wisdom from History's Greatest Wordsmiths* (New York: HarperCollins, 2004), p. 148.
10. Alan Dershowitz, *America on Trial: Inside the Legal Battles That Transformed Our Nation* (New York: Warner Books, 2004), p. 73.
11. Alan Dershowitz, *Blasphemy: How the Religious Right Is Hijacking Our Declaration of Independence* (Hoboken, NJ: John Wiley & Sons, 2007).
12. Letter to Roger Weightman, June 24, 1826, in *The Life and Selected Writings of Thomas Jefferson*, ed. Adrienne Koch and William Peden (New York: Modern Library, 1944), p. 729.
13. Several years ago I purchased a wonderful old pamphlet about the "pernicious practice of law," published by an acquaintance of Jefferson. The essays, signed "Honestus," were written by Benjamin Austin in 1786. They rail against dishonest lawyers of the day. They were published in 1814 and sent to Jefferson, who wrote to Austin in 1816, indicating some agreement with his points:
    Your favor of December 21st has been received, and I am first to thank you for the pamphlet it covered. The same description of persons which is the subject of that is so much multiplied here too, as to be almost a grievance, and by their numbers in the public councils, have wrested from the public hand the direction of the pruning knife.

3 Finding the Jefferson Letter

1. Adam Gopnick, "Family Business," *New Yorker* (January 14, 1991), p. 22.
2. Michael Thomas, "Volumes of Praise," *Quest* (October 2005), p. 145.
3. According to Silvio Bedini:
    On February 1, 1770, while young Thomas Jefferson was in Williamsburg practicing law and attending the meetings of the House of Burgesses, his family home, Shadwell, burned to the ground. Virtually nothing survived the blaze; all of his papers and those of his father perished with his books and other personal possessions. As he wrote to his friend John Page soon afterward, he had lost "every paper I had in the world and almost every book. On a reasonable estimate I calculate the cost of the books burned to have been £200 sterling. . . . Of the papers too of every kind I am utterly destitute. All of these, whether public or private, or business or amusement, have perished in the flames." *Thomas Jefferson and His Copying*

Machines (Charlottesville: University Press of Virginia, 1984), p. 1.

4. Thomas, "Volumes of Praise," p. 145.
5. Sara Nelson, "A Family Affair," *PW Book Life* (December 2005/January 2006): 26–28.
6. Gopnick, "Family Business," p. 22.
7. Gary Shapiro, "An Uptown Book Oasis," *New York Sun*, February 14, 2006, p. 16.
8. Dumas Malone, *Jefferson and His Time*, vol. 4 (Boston: Little, Brown, 1970), p. 5.
9. Stanley Griswold, *Overcoming Evil with Good: A Sermon, Delivered at Wallingford, Connecticut, March 11, 1801; before a Numerous Collection of the Friends of the Constitution, of Thomas Jefferson, President, and of Aaron Burr, Vice-President of the United States* (Hartford, CT: Elisha Babcock, 1801).
10. William Robinson, "Griswold, Stanley," in *Dictionary of American Biography*, ed. Dumas Malone (New York: Charles Scribner's Sons, 1932), vol. 8, p. 13.
11. Ibid.
12. In *Jefferson and Civil Liberties: The Darker Side*, Leonard Levy wrote:

    In brief the new libertarians advocated that only "injurious conduct," as manifested by "overt acts" or deeds, rather than words, might be criminally redressable. They did not refine this proposition except to recognize that the law of libel should continue to protect private reputation against malicious falsehoods. They would not even recognize that under certain circumstances words might immediately and directly incite criminal acts.

    The "new libertarians," according to Leonard Levy, included George Hay, John Thompson, Tunis Wortman, and James Madison. Levy excludes Jefferson from this list, claiming that "it is doubtful that the new libertarianism meant much to Jefferson for it scarcely altered his own thinking" (Cambridge, MA: Belknap Press, 1963), p. 54. At page 55, Levy believed that Jefferson refused to extend the overt-act test to political speech. At chapter 15, Jefferson's letter to Boardman shows, to the contrary, that he did.
13. Silvio Bedini, *Thomas Jefferson and His Copying Machines*, pp. 4–5.
14. Lester J. Cappon, ed., *The Adams-Jefferson Letters: The Complete Correspondence between Thomas Jefferson and Abigail and John Adams* (Chapel Hill: University of North Carolina Press, 1988).

15. Ibid.
16. Ibid.
17. See Larry Kramer and Lawrence Tribe, "The Supreme Court 2000 Term," *Harvard Law Review* 115, no.1 (November 2001): 6.
18. James Alexander, *A Brief Narrative of the Case and Trial of John Peter Zenger*, ed. Stanley Katz (Cambridge, MA: Belknap Press, 1972), p. 62.
19. Ibid.
20. James Morton Smith, *Freedom's Fetters; the Alien and Sedition Laws and American Civil Liberties* (Ithaca, NY: Cornell University Press, 1956), pp. 136, 140; footnote from original in Lester J. Cappon, ed., *The Adams-Jefferson Letters: The Complete Correspondence between Thomas Jefferson and Abigail and John Adams* (Chapel Hill: University of North Carolina Press, 1988).
21. Leonard Levy, *Jefferson and Civil Liberties*, pp. 28–31.
22. Barbara Oberg, ed., *The Papers of Thomas Jefferson*, Volume 30: *1 January 1798 to 31 January 1799* (Princeton, NJ: Princeton University Press, 2003), pp. 550–556.
23. Thomas Jefferson to Edward Carrington, January 16, 1787, *The Thomas Jefferson Papers Series 1, General Correspondence, 1651–1827* (Library of Congress).
24. Jefferson letter to Archibald Stuart, May 14, 1799, in John Kaminski, ed., *The Quotable Jefferson* (Princeton, NJ: Princeton University Press, 2006), p. 342.
25. Thomas Jefferson, first inaugural address, March 4, 1801. The Avalon Project, Yale Law School, www.yale.edu/lawweb/avalon/presiden/inaug/jefinau1.htm.
26. Jefferson letter to John Morvell, June 11, 1807, in Adrienne Koch and William Peden, eds., *The Life and Selected Writings of Thomas Jefferson* (New York: Modern Library, 1944).
27. Ibid., p. 582.
28. Jefferson letter to Walter Jones, January 2, 1814, in Koch and Peden, *The Life and Selected Writings of Thomas Jefferson*.
29. Kaminski, pp. xlviii, 498, 289.
30. Levy, *Jefferson and Civil Liberties*, p. 44.
31. Arthur Schlesinger, "Folly's Antidote," *New York Times*, January 1, 2007, p. A19.
32. Ibid.

4 The Provenance of the Jefferson-Boardman Letter

1. Letter from Martha J. King, associate editor, Papers of Thomas Jefferson, to Alan Dershowitz, September 12, 2006.

2. John Kaminski, ed., *The Quotable Jefferson* (Princeton, NJ: Princeton University Press, 2006), p. 248.

3. Ibid., p. 249.

4. Letter from Martha J. King to Alan Dershowitz, September 12, 2006.

5. Leonard Levy, *Jefferson and Civil Liberties: The Darker Side* (Cambridge, MA: Belknap Press, 1963), p. 171.

6. Adrienne Koch and William Peden, eds., *The Life and Selected Writings of Thomas Jefferson* (New York: Modern Library, 1944), p. 607.

7. Ibid., pp. 608–613.

8. As Silvio Bedini wrote in *Thomas Jefferson and His Copying Machines*:

> Jefferson's concern with the restoration of records and correspondence was not limited solely to his own papers. As a student at the College of William and Mary anticipating a legal career, he sought out the colony's earliest laws maintained in the Public Record Office in Williamsburg. He was appalled at their condition and transcribed a great number of them. He also collected printed and manuscript copies of others, wrapping and sewing fragile documents in oilcloth to protect them from the atmosphere. As he wrote in 1796 to his great friend and mentor George Wythe[:]
>
>> I observed that many of them were already lost, and many more on the point of being lost, as existing in only single copies in the hands of careful or curious individuals, on whose death they would probably be used for waste paper, I set myself therefore to work, to collect all which were then existing, in order that when the day would come in which the public should avert to the magnitude of their loss in these previous monuments of our property, and our history, a part of their regret might be spared by information that a portion had been saved from the wreck, which is worthy of their attention and preservation.
>
> Jefferson spared neither time nor cost in making this collection, which included copies of many of those documents which the British later destroyed. In 1807 he lent his collection to William Waller Henning for his compilation of *The Statutes at Large*, a massive work which brought to realization Jefferson's ambition to preserve by means of publication those records "from the worm, from the natural decay of the paper, from the accidents of fire, or those of removal when

it is necessary for any public purpose . . . [to avoid] ravages of fire and ferocious enemies."

In addition to destruction by fire and war, Jefferson realized that equal damage was done to public documents by neglect, which he considered to be even more intolerable for it implied a lack of concern about the heritage they contained. Nowhere was Jefferson's preoccupation more eloquently expressed than in a letter to Ebenezer Hazard, the historian who had copied the records of the United Colonies of New England and published them as his *Historical Collections*. Having learned of the project, in 1791 Jefferson borrowed the two manuscript volumes prior to their publication. Upon returning them, he wrote to Hazard: "Time and accident are committing daily havoc on the originals deposited in our public offices. The late war has done the work of centuries in this business. The lost cannot be recovered; but let us save what remains: not by vaults and locks which fence them from the public eye and use, in consigning them to the waste of time, but by such multiplication of copies, as shall place them beyond the reach of accident."

In this plea Jefferson anticipated the needs of not only historians and students but also of future solons who would seek precedents and guidance from the legislators and events of the past. Himself an avid reader of history from his youth to his final years, he was much more acutely aware than his less scholarly inclined contemporaries that the records of the colonies and those related to achieving and developing a new nation, as well as those produced in the daily business of government, would in time become important for future generations as a part of a national heritage which was then in its embryonic stage.

Charlottesville: University Press of Virginia, 1984, p. 2.

9. Letter to William Short, Monticello, New York, May 5, 1816, in John Kaminski, ed., *The Quotable Jefferson* (Princeton, NJ: Princeton University Press, 2006), p. 185.

10. Letter to William Johnson, Monticello, New York, June 12, 1823, ibid., pp. 184–185.

11. John Adams letter to Thomas Jefferson, July 12, 1822, in Lester J. Cappon, ed., *The Adams-Jefferson Letters: The Complete Correspondence between Thomas Jefferson and Abigail and John Adams* (Chapel Hill: University of North Carolina Press, 1988), p. 582.

12. The letter, along with all other letters, copies of which are in the possession of the Library of Congress or the Jefferson Collection at the University of Virginia, will eventually be published as part of a multivolume set of the complete writings of Thomas Jefferson. Ibid., 484.

13. Quoted in Kaminski, *The Quotable Jefferson*, p. 264.
14. It is likely that this spelling was a homophone error, given the standard usage at that time. See definitions of "too" and "to" in Samuel Johnson, *The Synonymous, Etymological, and Pronouncing English Dictionary* (London: T. Gillet, 1805).
15. Joyce Appleby and Terence Ball, eds., *Jefferson: Political Writings* (Cambridge, MA: Cambridge Univeristy Press, 1999), p. xiv.
16. Kaminski, *The Quotable Jefferson*, p. 272.
17. *Abrams v. United States*, 250 U.S. 616, 630.
18. Levy, *Jefferson and Civil Liberties*, p. 54.
19. Ibid., p. 53.
20. Ibid., p. xv.
21. Alan Dershowitz, *The Genesis of Justice: Ten Stories of Biblical Injustice That Led to the Ten Commandments and Modern Law* (New York: Warner Books, 2000), pp. 16–17.
22. As Martha King wrote in a letter to me, September 12, 2006:
    Evidently there were also other letters exchanged between Boardman and TJ, copies of which have not been found. We know of their existence, however, because of Jefferson's meticulous recordkeeping. In his epistolary record, a two-column register of letters written and received, referred to by us as "SJL" (summary journal of letters), Jefferson indicated the following items not found by us: Boardman to TJ, 28 Apr. 1801 from New Milford and received on 8 May 1801; Jefferson to Boardman, 28 June 1801; and Boardman to Jefferson, 30 Nov. 1806, from New Milford, Conn., recorded as received 9 Dec. 1806.

5 Where We Have Come since 1826

1. Quoted in Dershowitz, *America Declares Independence* (Hoboken, NJ: John Wiley & Sons, 2003), pp. 18–20. See Lester J. Cappon, ed., *The Adams-Jefferson Letters: The Complete Correspondence between Thomas Jefferson and Abigail and John Adams* (Chapel Hill: University of North Carolina Press, 1988).
2. To read this letter, visit the Library of Congress Web site at www.loc.gov/exhibits/declara/declara4.html, accessed May 2, 2007.
3. *New York Times Co. v. Sullivan*, 376 U.S. 254 at 276 (1964). Justice Brennan wrote the opinion of the court.
4. Quoted in Alan Dershowitz, *America Declares Independence* p. 125.
5. Michael Green, *Freedom, Union, and Power: Lincoln and His Party during the Civil War* (New York: Fordham University Press, 2004), p. 186. Also see James Randall, *Constitutional*

Problems under Lincoln (New York: D. Appleton & Company, 1926), p. 500.

6. Addressing Congress on July 4, 1864, as cited in Green, *Freedom, Union, and Power*.

7. As Paul Escott wrote in *Military Necessity: Civil-Military Relations in the Confederacy*:

But there were infringements on speech and on individuals' rights and freedom as well. As the military guarded against those who might be disloyal, it scrutinized dissidents, critics of the administration, or suspected Unionists. Military commanders sometimes called on citizens to inform on others who might be security risks, and they imposed censorship in Richmond, Charleston, New Orleans, and Vicksburg. The orders of censorship went beyond concern for protecting the secrecy of troop movements. For example, General Earl Van Dorn ordered newspapers to publish nothing "calculated to impair confidence in any of the commanding officers." Most seriously, thousands of people were arrested and held, including an unknown number for short periods of time. . . . Army officers needed no encouragement to put perceived military needs above individuals' civil rights.

Westport, CT: Praeger Security International, 2006, pp. 89–90.

8. Many of those prosecuted were Jews, Italians, and other minority immigrant groups. Jefferson apparently had mixed views with regard to Jews. Though he opposed their persecution, he characterized them as having "a perversity of character" (letter to John Taylor, June 1, 1758) and described their religion in the following terms:

II. Jews. 1. Their system was Deism; that is, the belief in one only God. But their ideas of him and of his attributes were degrading and injurious.

2. Their Ethics were not only imperfect, but often irreconcilable with the sound dictates of reason and morality, as they respect intercourse with those around us; and repulsive and anti-social, as respecting other nations. They needed reformation, therefore, in an eminent degree.

III. Jesus. In this state of things among the Jews, Jesus appeared. His parentage was obscure; his condition poor; his education null; his natural endowments great; his life correct and innocent: he was meek, benevolent, patient, firm, disinterested, and of the sublimest eloquence.

I. He corrected the Deism of the Jews, confirming them in their belief of one only God, and giving them juster notions of his attributes and government.

2. his moral doctrines, relating to kindred and friends, were

more pure and perfect than those of the most correct of the
philosophers and greatly more so than those of the Jews; and
they went far beyond both in inculcating universal philan-
thropy, not only to kindred and friends, to neighbors and
countrymen, but to all mankind gathering all into one family,
under the bonds of love, charity, peace, common wants and
common aids. A development of this head will evince the
peculiar superiority of the system of Jesus over all others.
  3. The precepts of philosophy, and of the Hebrew code,
laid hold of actions only. He pushed his scrutinies into the
heart of man[;] erected his tribunal in the region of his
thoughts, and purified the waters at the fountain head.
  4. He taught, emphatically, the doctrines of a future state,
which was either doubted, or disbelieved by the Jews; and
wielded it with efficacy, as an important incentive, supplemen-
tary to the other motives to moral conduct.
Quoted in Joyce Appleby and Terence Ball, eds., *Thomas Jefferson: Political Writings* (New York: Cambridge Univeristy Press,
1999), pp. 268–270. Jefferson was apparently more familiar with
the Jewish Bible than with the rabbinic and Talmudic literature.
His stereotypes were somewhat typical for his era.

9. Griffin Fariello, *Red Scare: Memories of the American Inquisition:
An Oral History* (New York: W. W. Norton, 1995), p. 353. See
also Charles McCormick, *Seeing Reds: Federal Surveillance of
Radicals in the Pittsburgh Mill District* (Pittsburgh: University of
Pittsburgh Press, 1997).

10. Christopher Hitchens, "Jefferson's Quran," *Slate* (January 9,
2007), www.slate.com/id/2157314/, last accessed May 2, 2007.

11. Quoted in Michael B. Oren, *Power, Faith, and Fantasy: America
in the Middle East, 1776 to the Present* (New York: Norton,
2007), p. 31.

12. Ibid., p. 32.

13. Ibid., p. 29.

14. As I introduced the concept in my book *Rights from Wrongs*:
I propose a third way—an experiential approach based on nurture rather than nature. This approach builds a theory of rights
from the bottom up, not from the top down. It constructs this
theory by examining the history of injustices, inducing certain
experiential lessons, and advocating rights based on those lessons. I therefore come down squarely on the side of nurture,
rather than nature, as the primary source of our rights. I would
prefer the term "nurtural rights" over "natural rights" if it
were more pleasing to the ear. . . . [T]he major new insight
offered by my theory of rights is that it is not necessary to have

a conception of the "perfect," the "best," or even the good society in order to decide whether rights in general, or certain rights in particular, will serve the ends of a given society. . . . It is enough to have a conception—or a consensus—about the very bad society, and about the wrongs that made it so. Based on this experience with wrongs, rights can be designed to prevent (or at least slow down) the recurrence of such wrongs. New York: Basic Books, 2004, p. 6.

15. John P. Kaminski, ed., *The Quotable Jefferson* (Princeton, NJ: Princeton University Press, 2006), p. 231.

16. The Fourth Amendment—in the news recently because of the exposure of the Bush administration's program of warrantless wiretapping—grants citizens protection against "unreasonable searches and seizures." The Fifth Amendment—something of a grab-bag of rights—provides for a grand jury, protects against "double-jeopardy," allows the accused to decline to testify against himself or herself, and stipulates that no citizen shall be "deprived of life, liberty, or property, without due process of law." The Sixth Amendment provides the accused with the right to a "speedy and public trial," an impartial jury of his or her peers, information regarding the charges against him or her, the right to face his or her accuser, the right to call witnesses in his or her defense, and the right to legal counsel. The Eighth Amendment reads simply: "Excessive bail shall not be required, nor excessive fines imposed, nor cruel and unusual punishments inflicted."

While the text of these amendments has been the same since the adoption of the Bill of Rights in 1791, the interpretation of them has varied widely throughout American history. For one, the range of situations in which the first ten amendments apply has evolved dramatically; initially, the enumerated rights were thought to limit only the Federal government. Over the ensuing two hundred years, nearly all of them (except the right to a grand jury) have been applied to the states by the Supreme Court through the Fourteenth Amendment, a doctrine called "selective incorporation."

The drive toward incorporation—as well as toward a more broad reading of the enumerated criminal rights described previously—reached its zenith during the Warren Court of the 1960s. Beginning with the application of the Fourth Amendment exclusionary rule in *Mapp v. Ohio* (1961), the Court expanded and incorporated criminal rights, including the Eighth Amendment (in *Robinson v. California*, 1962), the Fifth Amendment right against self-incrimination (*Malloy v. Hogan*, 1964), portions of the Sixth Amendment (the right to face one's accuser, in *Pointer v. Texas*, 1965, and the right to a speedy trial, in *Klopfer v. North Carolina*, 1967), the right to a court-appointed counsel (*Gideon v. Wainwright*, 1963), and the right to be made aware of one's rights (*Miranda v. Arizona*, 1966). Morton Horwitz, *The Warren Court and the Pursuit of Justice* (New York: Hill and Wang, 1998), pp. 94–95. The Court took quite a bit of heat for these rulings, which were seen as siding with criminals during the turbulent Nixon years; as a result, the Court began to retreat from its stance on criminal rights. In the years since the Warren Court, the Supreme Court has become less sympathetic to criminal rights. For more, see Horwitz, *The Warren Court and the Pursuit of Justice*.

17. See Dershowitz, *Rights from Wrongs*.
18. See Kaminski, pp. xlviii, 289, 498.
19. Leonard Levy, *Jefferson and Civil Liberties: The Darker Side* (Cambridge, MA: Belknap Press, 1963), p. 47.
20. One major British ruling that reflects Jefferson's view is *Irving v. Penguin Books Ltd & Lipstadt* (1996). David Irving, a Holocaust denier, claimed that the author Deborah Lipstadt libeled him in her book *Denying the Holocaust*. Irving alleged that passages in Lipstadt's book "vandalised [his] legitimacy as an historian." In his decision, the judge for the Crown painstakingly examined the history of the Holocaust and the verity of the claims by both Lipstadt in regard to Irving and Irving with regard to the Holocaust. Finding Lipstadt's claims regarding Irving's writings and opinions to be true—and Irving's twisting and omission of the facts of the Holocaust to be false—the judge found in favor of Lipstadt (and truth). (To read the judgment, visit www.hmcourts-service.gov.uk/judgmentsfiles/j22/queen_irving.htm, accessed May 2, 2007.)

More recently, the House of Lords ruled that the media have the right to print allegations that might be considered defamatory of public figures, so long as doing so is in the public interest. The British press hailed this ruling as bringing "English law more into line with the freedom enjoyed by the US media." To read the October 2006 ruling, see http://www.timesonline.co.uk/article/0,,200-2398969,00.html, accessed May 2, 2007, and to read the *London Times* story reporting the verdict, see www.business.timesonline.co.uk/tol/business/law/public/article668352.ece, accessed May 2, 2007.

21. This was established in the 1964 case *New York Times Co. v.*

Sullivan. This was the first case where the Supreme Court applied the First Amendment to state libel laws. The suit was brought against the *New York Times* because it published an advertisement that "included statements, some of which were false, about police action allegedly directed against students who participated in a civil rights demonstration and against a leader of the civil rights movement" (376 U.S. 254, syllabus). The false statements, according to a public official mentioned in the advertisement, were libelous. Although some of the statements were false, the Court held that "the rule of law applied by the Alabama courts is constitutionally deficient for failure to provide the safeguards for freedom of speech and of the press that are required by the First and Fourteenth Amendments in a libel action brought by a public official against critics of his official conduct" (264). The Court recognized "that erroneous statement is inevitable in free debate, and that it must be protected if the freedoms of expression are to have the 'breathing space' that they 'need . . . to survive'" (271–272). The right to be wrong, as long as the mistake is not intentional or malicious, is vital to popular sovereignty.

22. Justice Lewis Powell determined that "[u]nder the First Amendment there is no such thing as a false idea; however pernicious an opinion may seem, its correction depends not on the conscience of judges and juries but on the competition of other ideas" (418 U.S. 323 at 339). The courts have also ruled that groups cannot be defamed and that false history cannot be challenged. Thus absurd claims—such as that the Holocaust did not occur—can be made with impunity.

6 Jefferson's First Argument: An Expressed Opinion Can Never Constitute an Overt Act

1. Thomas Jefferson, *The Writings of Thomas Jefferson*, vol. 1, ed. Andrew A. Lipscomb (Washington, DC: Thomas Jefferson Memorial Association, 1903), pp. 226–227.

2. From an 1824 letter to John Adams: "Where did we get the ten commandments? The book indeed give them to us verbatim, but where did it get them? For itself tells us they were written by the finger of God on tables of stone, which were destroyed by Moses; it specifies those on the second set of tables in different form and substance, but still without saying how the other were recovered. But the whole history of these books is so defective and doubtful, that it seems vain to attempt minute inquiry into it; and such tricks have been played with their text, and with the other texts

of other books relating to them, that we have a right from that cause to entertain much doubt what parts of them are genuine." Quoted in Alan Dershowitz, *America Declares Independence* (Hoboken, NJ: John Wiley & Sons, 2003), pp. 28–29.

3. James Willard Hurst, *The Law of Treason in the United States: Collected Essays* (Westport, CT: Greenwood Publishing Corp., 1971), cited in *The Founders' Constitution*, Volume 4, Article 3, Section 3, Clauses 1 and 2, Document 1. See http://presspubs .uchicago.edu/founders/documents/a3_3_1–2s1.html (Chicago: University of Chicago Press, 1987).

4. William Blackstone, *Commentaries on the Laws of England: A Facsimile of the First Edition of 1765–1769* (Chicago: University of Chicago Press, 1979). From *The Founders' Constitution*, Volume 4, Article 3, Section 3, Clauses 1 and 2, Document 8. See http://press-pubs.uchicago.edu/founders/ documents/a3_3_1–2s8.html, accessed May 2, 2007 (Chicago: University of Chicago Press, 1987).

5. John O'Brien, "City Man Admits Threat to Bush," *Syracuse Post-Standard*, April 12, 2001, p. B1.

6. This empirical argument has been disputed. See Alan Dershowitz, *Shouting Fire: Civil Liberties in a Turbulent Age* (Boston: Little, Brown, 2002), pp 168–169.

7. Richard Dawkins, in his book *The God Delusion* (New York: Houghton Mifflin, 2006), the aggressively atheistic Oxford University professor, discusses the Bible:

There are two ways in which scripture might be a source of morals or rules for living. One is by direct instruction, for example through the Ten Commandments, which are the subject of such bitter contention in the culture wars of America's boondocks. The other is by example: God, or some other biblical character, might serve as—to use the contemporary jargon—a role model. Both scriptural routes, if followed through religiously (the adverb is used in its metaphoric sense but with an eye to its origin), encourage a system of morals which any civilized modern person, whether religious or not, would find—I can put it no more gently—obnoxious. . . . But unfortunately it is this same weird volume that religious zealots hold up to us as the inerrant source of our morals and rules for living. . . . However misguided we may think [terrorists], they are motivated, like the Christian murderers of abortion doctors, by what they perceive to be righteousness, faithfully pursuing what their religion tells them. They are not psychotic; they are religious idealists who, by their own lights, are rational. They perceive their acts to be good, not because of some warped personal idiosyncrasy, and not because they have been possessed by Satan, but because they have been brought up, from the cradle, to have total and unquestioning *faith*.

8. From *Gitlow v. New York*, 268 U.S. 652 (1925), at 673.
9. Tim Ross, "Schools Ignore Holocaust; Teachers Don't Want to Cause Offense," *Daily Post* (Liverpool), April 2, 2007, p. 11.
10. *Whitney v. California*, 274 U.S. 357 (1927), at 377.
11. John Foley, ed., *The Jeffersonian Cyclopedia* (New York: Funk & Wagnall's Co., 1900), p. 811.
12. As Jefferson wrote in a letter to Benjamin Banneker, Philadelphia, August 30, 1791: "No body wishes more than I do to see such proofs as you exhibit, that nature has given to our black brethren, talents equal to those of the other colors of men, & that the appearance of a want of them is owing merely to the degraded condition of their existence both in Africa and America. I can add with truth that no body wishes more ardently to see a good system commenced for raising the condition both of their body & mind to what it ought to be, as fast as the imbecility of their present existence, and other circumstances which cannot be neglected, will admit." Found in John P. Kaminski, ed., *The Quotable Jefferson* (Princeton, NJ: Princeton University Press, 2006), p. 351.
13. Some have argued that to deny the Holocaust is to encourage another one; one such person is the German justice minister Brigitte Zypries. Regarding criticism of laws against Holocaust denial, she said, "We believe there are limits to freedom of expression. . . . We should not wait until it comes to deeds. We must act against the intellectual pathbreakers of the crime." From "Slippery Slope," *Economist* (January 27, 2007).

7 Jefferson's Second Argument: If Conscience Is the Umpire, Then Each Judge's Conscience Will Govern

1. Thomas Jefferson letter to Albert Gallatin, January 13, 1807, in John P. Kaminski, ed., *The Quotable Jefferson* (Princeton, NJ: Princeton University Press, 2006), p. 396.
2. Thomas Jefferson to Thomas Paine, 1789, *The Papers of Thomas Jefferson* (Princeton, NJ: Princeton University Press, 2003), chap. 15, p. 269.
3. See "good faith," *West's Encyclopedia of American Law* (Minneapolis/St. Paul, MN: West Publishing, 1998).
4. See Linda Greenhouse, "Case of the Dwindling Docket Mystified the Supreme Court," *New York Times*, December 7, 2006, p. A1.

8 Jefferson's Third Argument: "We Have Nothing to Fear from the Demoralizing Reasonings of Some, if Others Are Left Free to Demonstrate Their Errors"

1. As I noted in *Rights from Wrongs*, common misconceptions about law and policy are often propagated by the news outlets—the ideological sources, in particular. For example:

   The 2004 documentary *Outfoxed: Rupert Murdoch's War on Journalism* helped to publicize a study that showed that viewers who received most of their news from the Fox News Channel held misperceptions about current events far more frequently than did those who received most of their news from PBS or NPR. This PIPA/Knowledge Networks Poll, titled "Misperceptions, the Media, and the Iraq War" [2003] . . . found that 67% of those who get most of their news from Fox have the impression that the United States has found clear evidence that Saddam Hussein was working closely with al Qaeda, while only 16% of those who received most of their news from PBS or NPR had this misconception. P. 246, n. 1.

2. Even Senator John McCain, who has been a vocal critic of the use of torture, will not make that trade-off. He instead insists that torture doesn't work, because by so insisting he eliminates the choice of evils:

   We should not torture or treat inhumanely terrorists we have captured. The abuse of prisoners harms, not helps, our war effort. In my experience, abuse of prisoners often produces bad intelligence because under torture a person will say anything he thinks his captors want to hear—whether it is true or false—if he believes it will relieve his suffering. I was once physically coerced to provide my enemies with the names of the members of my flight squadron, information that had little if any value to my enemies as actionable intelligence. But I did not refuse, or repeat my insistence that I was required under the Geneva Conventions to provide my captors only with my name, rank and serial number. Instead, I gave them the names of the Green Bay Packers' offensive line, knowing that providing them false information was sufficient to suspend the abuse. It seems probable to me that the terrorists we interrogate under less than humane standards of treatment are also likely to resort to deceptive answers that are perhaps less provably false than that which I once offered.

   John McCain, "Torture's Terrible Toll," *Newsweek* (November 21, 2005), p. 34.

3. On federalism: Although Jefferson was wary to grow the power of the federal government at the expense of states' rights and so

doubted the constitutionality of the Lousiana Purchase, he purchased it anyway and more than doubled the size of the new republic.

On an American military: David Stout of the *New York Times* wrote that Jefferson changed his views on the citizenry's engagement with the military. Stout wrote: "'The spirit of this country is totally adverse to a large military force,' Thomas Jefferson wrote in 1807. . . . Jefferson, too, changed his views. 'We must train and classify the whole of our male citizens and make military instruction a regular part of collegiate education,' he wrote in 1813, when the United States was fighting Britain. 'We can never be safe till this is done.'" "The Nation: An Army as Good as Its People, and Vice Versa," *New York Times*, July 26, 1998, p. D4.

On blacks' intelligence: Jefferson certainly was open to changing his views on the "inferiority" of blacks. In his *Notes on the State of Virginia* (1787), Jefferson wrote:

To our reproach it must be said, that though for a century and a half we have had under our eyes the races of black and of red men, they have never yet been viewed by us as subjects of natural history. [A]dvance it therefore as a suspicion only, that the blacks, whether originally a distinct race, or made distinct by time and circumstances, are inferior to the whites in the endowments both of body and mind. It is not against experience to suppose, that different species of the same genus, or varieties of the same species, may possess different qualifications.

Thomas Jefferson, *Notes on the State of Virginia*, 1787, p. 270, University of Virginia Library Text Center, http://etext .virginia.edu/etcbin/toccer-new2?id=JefVirg.sgm&images= images/modeng&data=/texts/english/modeng/parsed& tag=public&part=all, accessed May 7, 2007.

Yet in a letter written to Benjamin Banneker, a free black mathematician and surveyor who sent Jefferson a copy of his almanac to change Jefferson's views on the supposed inferiority of blacks, Jefferson wrote that "[N]o body wishes more than I do to see such proofs as you exhibit, that nature has given to our black brethren, talents equal to those of the other colors of men." Thomas Jefferson to Benjamin Banneker, August 30, 1791.

9 Jefferson's Fourth Argument: "The Law Stands Ready to Punish the First Criminal Act Produced by the False Reasoning"

1. See Justice Antonin Scalia's dissent in *Hamdi v. Rumsfeld*, 542 U.S. 507 (2004), at 560. The British standard required an overt

act, though with exceptions. As Sir Matthew Hale, in *History of the Pleas of the Crown 1736*, wrote, "Therefore tho this be regularly true, that words alone make not treason or an overt-act . . . it hath these allays and exceptions," which include the aforementioned "compassing," words "that are expressly menacing the death or destruction of the king," and "an assembling together to consider how they may kill the king." From Sir Matthew Hale, *Historia Placitorum Coronae. The History of the Pleas of the Crown*, 2 vols., ed. by Sollom Emlyn (London, 1736 [reprint. Classical English Law Texts. London: Professional Books, Ltd., 1971]), quoted in *The Founders' Constitution*, 4 vols. (Chicago: University of Chicago Press, 1987). Others, such as Sir Michael Foster, in his *Discourse on High Treason* (1762), further mention "the Entering into Measures in concert with Foreigners or others in order to an Invasion of the Kingdom, or going into a Foreign Country, or even Purposing to go thither to that End *and taking any Steps in order thereto*, these Offences are Overt-Acts of Compassing the King's Death." (*The Founders' Constitution*.)

2. Inspired by Seneca's *Epigrams*, Book IV, Ep. 5:
   Prosperum ac felix scelus
   Virtus vocatur
   (Successful and fortunate crime is called virtue).
   Seneca: Herc. Furens, ii. 250.

   John Bartlett, compiler, *Familiar Quotations*, 10th ed., rev. and enl. by Nathan Haskell Dole (Boston: Little, Brown, 1919); Bartleby.com 2000, www.bartleby.com/100/, accessed January 16, 2007.

3. In 1969, during the domestic turmoil roiling over the Vietnam War, the United States prosecuted the influential pediatrician (not to mention the presidential candidate and Olympic gold medalist) Dr. Benjamin Spock for conspiracy against the United States, citing his activities in protesting the military draft. Spock, along with the Yale chaplain Reverend William Sloane Coffin Jr. and a number of others, had signed a letter calling for disobedience in the face of the draft, delivered speeches at a press conference in support of the letter, and participated in a draft-card burning demonstration in Washington, D.C., among other things. It was alleged that the "defendants, and others known and unknown, conspired to 'counsel, aid and abet diverse Selective Service registrants to neglect, fail, refuse and evade service in the armed forces of the United States and all other duties required of registrants under the Universal Military Training and Service Act

. . . [and conspired to] unlawfully, willfully and knowingly hinder and interfere, by any means, with the administration of the Universal Military Training and Service Act.'"
See 416 F.2d 165, 1969, at 168. They were convicted and appealed to the U.S. Circuit Court of Appeals for the First Circuit, where the lower court judgment was reversed. The judges found the necessity for a careful balancing of the government's interest in maintaining an army in wartime against the rights of free speech and association, which the court stated "are of such importance that they must prevail if the government's interest in deterring substantive crimes before they take place is insubstantial, or there is a 'less restrictive alternative' by which the substantive evil may be prevented" (at 170). Under the criteria for conspiracy—including evidence of agreement, whether the agreement contemplated or included illegal activity, and whether the individuals adhered to that illegality—the judges found that Spock's conviction must be overturned because of a lack of evidence of specific intent and illegal activity beyond his right to free speech. The government ultimately dropped the charges. When I was a young lawyer, I played a small role in the *Spock* case, assisting the defense.

4. Leonard Levy, *Jefferson and Civil Liberties: The Darker Side* (Cambride, MA: Belknap Press, 1963), pp. 171–172.
5. Alan Dershowitz, *The Best Defense* (New York: Random House, 1982), p. 215.
6. John Kaminski, ed., *The Quotable Jefferson* (Princeton, NJ: Princeton University Press, 2006), p. 150.

10 Jefferson's Fifth Argument: "These Are Safer Correctives than the Conscience of a Judge"

1. Quoted in Sanford Levinson, *Our Undemocratic Constitution: Where the Constitution Goes Wrong (and How We the People Can Correct It)* (New York: Oxford University Press, 2006), p. ix.
2. See *New York Times Co. v. Sullivan*, 376 U.S. 254 at 276 (1964).
3. Babylonian Talmud, Baba Mezia, p. 59b.

11 Jefferson's Views on the "Terrorism" of His Era

1. See Frank Lambert, *The Barbary Wars: American Independence in the Atlantic World* (New York: Hill and Wang, 2005), p. 118.
2. An option—though extraordinarily objectionable to a moral society—is what the Nazis called *sippenhaft*, or the punishment of

kin. This form of collective punishment would likely be an effective deterrent to suicide bombers, who cannot themselves pay for their crimes. I wrote more about this in *Why Terrorism Works: Understanding the Threat, Responding to the Challenge* (New Haven, CT: Yale University Press, 2002), pp. 117 and 173.

3. See Josh Gerstein, "Gingrich: Free Speech Should Be Curtailed to Fight Terrorism," *New York Sun*, November 29, 2006, p. 4.
4. See *The Making of a Martyr*, a 1967 film by Brooke Goldstein.
5. John Kaminski, ed., *The Quotable Jefferson* (Princeton, NJ: Princeton University Press, 2006), pp. 164–166.
6. Ibid., p. 231.

12 Jefferson's Actions in the Burr Case

1. Herbert Parmet and Marie Hecht, *Aaron Burr: Portrait of an Ambitious Man* (London: Macmillan, 1967), p. 287.
2. As Leonard Levy wrote in *Jefferson and Civil Liberties: The Darker Side*:

   Jefferson's handling of the interrogation and proceedings against Dr. Eric Bollman illuminated his conduct in the case. Bollman, who was one of Burr's principal aides, had been illegally arrested by the military and transported from New Orleans to the East to stand trial for treason. Escorted from prison by a squad of soldiers to be interviewed by the President and the Secretary of State, Bollman was eager to talk. Jefferson expected to get from him a full confession of Burr's treasonable plans. But the prisoner denied that there had been any conspiracy to seize New Orleans or to sever the West from the Union. He confessed that the object of the plot was to conquer Mexico and urged that the United States declare war on Spain, a measure that would have been immensely popular in the West. Bollman admitted that there had been a good deal of talk about a revolution in Louisiana, but all for the purpose of duping the Spanish by directing their attention from Burr's true objective.

   Bollman's confession had been given after the President had voluntarily assured him that nothing he said would be used as evidence to incriminate him. Though Madison had taken notes, Jefferson requested Bollman to put his remarks in writing. The President's letter offered "*his word of honour* that they shall never be used against himself [Bollman], and *that the paper shall never go out of his hand*." Bollman promptly furnished the President with a signed statement of almost twenty pages.

   Within a month, Chief Justice Marshall freed Bollman on a

writ of habeas corpus, ruling that there was no evidence to warrant his being held on a charge of treason. But the President was not finished with Bollman whom he meant to use as a witness against Burr, or, failing that, to imprison. When the case for an indictment against the archconspirator was prepared, the President sent Bollman's signed statement to the United States attorney, George Hay, in Richmond. Noting that Bollman's statement had been made with the assurance that it "should never be used *against himself*," Jefferson informed Hay that it would be useful "that you may know how to examine him, and draw everything from him." If Bollman lied on the stand, Hay "should go as far as to ask him whether he did not say so and so to Mr. Madison and myself." To induce Bollman to testify, Jefferson enclosed a pardon. If Bollman refused to appear as a witness, he was to be taken immediately into custody. A week later, Jefferson modified his instructions to Hay. "On further reflection," he declared, "I think you may go farther, if he prevaricates grossly, and shrew the paper to him, and ask if it is not his hand-writing, and confront him by its contents." (Cambridge, MA: Belknap Press, 1963), pp. 72–73.

3. Ibid., p. 71.
4. Alan Dershowitz, introduction to J. J. Coombs, *The Trial of Aaron Burr* (New York: Notable Trials Library, 1992), p. i.
5. Ibid.
6. James Parton, *The Life and Times of Aaron Burr* (London: Mason, 1858), p. 340.
7. Mardy Grothe, *Oxymoronica* (New York: HarperCollins, 2004), p. 142.
8. Quotes from Parmet and Hecht, *Aaron Burr*.
9. "For a man of his vigor, the prospect of being disenfranchised in New York and hanged in New Jersey only spurred attempts to spread his talents elsewhere." Ibid., p. 233.
10. Reprinted in the *Evening Post* (New York), February 6, 1805; cited in Jerry Knudson, "The Jeffersonian Assault on the Federalist Judiciary, 1802–1805; Political Forces and Press Reaction," *American Journal of Legal History* 14, no. 1 (January 1970): 72.
11. Coombs, *Trial of Aaron Burr*, p. 140.
12. Adrienne Koch and William Peden, eds., *The Life and Selected Writings of Thomas Jefferson* (New York: Random House, 1944), p. 585.
13. Thomas Jefferson letter to Robert Livingston, March 24, 1807, quoted in John P. Kaminski, ed., *The Quotable Jefferson* (Princeton, NJ: Princeton University Press, 2006), p. 402.
14. Groth, *Oxymoronica*, p. 14.

15. Parton, *The Life and Times of Aaron Burr*, pp. 456–457.
16. Levy, *Jefferson and Civil Liberties*, p. 75.
17. Coombs, *Trial of Aaron Burr*, pp. 136–137.
18. Ibid., from the introduction by Alan Dershowitz.
19. Ibid., p. 349.
20. Albert Beveridge, *The Life of John Marshall*, vol. 3 (Boston: Houghton Mifflin, 1916), p. 345.
21. *Ex parte Milligan*, 71 U.S. 2 (1866), at 125.
22. Sherrill Halbert, "The Suspension of the Writ of Habeas Corpus by President Lincoln," *American Journal of Legal History* 2, no. 2 (April 1958): 101.
23. In his second inaugural address, Jefferson devoted considerable attention to condemning the press:

    During this course of administration, and in order to disturb it, the artillery of the press has been leveled against us, charged with whatsoever its licentiousness could devise or dare. These abuses of an institution so important to freedom and science, are deeply to be regretted, inasmuch as they tend to lessen its usefulness, and to sap its safety; they might, indeed, have been corrected by the wholesome punishments reserved and provided by the laws of the several States against falsehood and defamation; but public duties more urgent press on the time of public servants, and the offenders have therefore been left to find their punishment in the public indignation. . . . No inference is here intended, that the laws, provided by the State against false and defamatory publications, should not be enforced; he who has time, renders a service to public morals and public tranquility, in reforming these abuses by the salutary coercions of the law. Joyce Appleby and Terence Ball, eds., *Jefferson's Political Writings* (New York: Cambridge University Press, 1999), pp. 533–534.

13 Jefferson's Views on Torture, Habeas Corpus, and Other Issues Currently Debated in the Context of Terrorism

1. Leonard Levy, *Jefferson and Civil Liberties: The Darker Side* (Cambridge, MA: Belknap Press, 1963), 406–409.
2. On May 26, 1810, Thomas Jefferson wrote to John Tyler:

    The opinion seems to be that Blackstone is to us what the Alcoran is to the Mahometans, that everything which is necessary is in him, and what is not in him is not necessary. I still lend my counsel and books to such young students as will fix themselves in the neighborhood. Coke's institutes and reports are their first, and Blackstone their last book, after an intermediate course of two or three years. It is nothing more than an

elegant digest of what they will then have acquired from the real fountains of the law. Now men are born scholars, lawyers, doctors; in our day this was confined to poets.
From *The Thomas Jefferson Papers Series 1, General Correspondence, 1651–1827* (Library of Congress).

3. In his autobiographic fragment, Jefferson wrote at length about the independence of the judiciary. See Thomas Jefferson, July 27, 1821, Autobiography Draft Fragment, January 6 through July 27, *The Thomas Jefferson Papers Series 1, General Correspondence, 1651–1827.*

4. John Kaminski, ed., *The Quotable Jefferson* (Princeton, NJ: Princeton University Press, 2006), p. 59.

5. Adrienne Koch and William Peden, eds., *The Life and Selected Writings of Thomas Jefferson* (New York: Random House, 1944), p. 451.

6. Thomas Jefferson's letter to James Madison, December 20, 1787.

7. According to Albert Beveridge, who was John Marshall's biographer, Jefferson may have been worried by an "account of Burr's intention to assassinate Jefferson" (vol. 3, p. 345). He then apparently orchestrated "an extreme and violent step."
   On Friday, January 23, 1807, the day after the President's Special Message denouncing Burr had been read in the Senate, Senator Giles, who, it should be repeated, was Jefferson's personal representative in that body, actually moved the appointment of a committee to draft a bill "to suspend the privilege of the writ of habeas corpus." Quickly Giles himself reported the measure, the Senate suspended its rules, and the bill was hurriedly passed, only Bayard of Delaware voting against it. More astounding still, Giles recommended, and the Senate adopted, a special message to the House, stating the Senate's action, "which they think expedient to communicate to you in confidence," and asking the popular branch of Congress to pass the Senate bill without delay. Immediately after the House convened on Monday, January 26, Senator Samuel Smith of Maryland appeared on the floor and delivered this "confidence message," together with the Senate bill, which provided that "in all cases, where any person or persons, charged on oath with treason, misprision of treason, or other high crime or misdemeanor . . . shall be arrested or imprisoned . . . the privilege of the writ of habeas corpus shall be . . . suspended, for and during the term of three months."
   Ultimately the measure was defeated.

8. See Alan Dershowitz, *Shouting Fire: Civil Liberties in a Turbulent Age* (Boston: Little, Brown, 2002), pp. 416–430:

"But what if we faced a situation similar to the one that confronts the Canadian government, where those fomenting violence were well known to the authorities, but the absence of admissible evidence made conviction impossible? Wouldn't you be tempted," I asked [Deputy Attorney General Richard] Kleindienst, "to invoke extraordinary powers of temporary detention in order to break the back of the movement?"

"We wouldn't have to," he assured me. "There is enough play at the joints of our existing criminal law—enough flexibility—so that if we really felt that we had to pick up the leaders of a violent uprising, we could. We would find something to charge them with and we would be able to hold them that way for a while."

Mr. Kleindienst's last remark reminded me of something the Canadian attorney general, John Turner, had told me during a conference he recently convened to evaluate his country's experience under the War Measures Act: "In a certain sense, it is a credit to the civil liberties of a country that it has to invoke extraordinary powers to cope with a real emergency. Some countries have these powers at their disposal all the time."

But whether a country has to invoke extraordinary powers or whether it already has sufficient powers at its disposal tells us little about the actual condition of liberty within its borders. Every legal system has its "stretch points," its flexible areas capable of expansion and contraction depending on the exigencies of the situation. The "stretch points" in our own system include broad police and prosecutorial discretion; vaguely defined offenses (such as disorderly conduct); inchoate crimes (which may also be vaguely defined, like conspiracy); and denial of pretrial release (which can sometimes result in confinement exceeding a year). Some systems employ such devices as common-law (judge-made) crimes, ex post facto (after the fact) legislation, and emergency powers, to achieve similar results. As Attorney General Turner put it: "When placed against the wall, most governments act more alike than differently; they do what they have to do to survive." There are, nevertheless, important differences in the manner by which governments respond to perceived emergencies. Some will take considerable risks to their security in order to preserve a maximum of liberty; while others will become harshly repressive at the slightest threat—real or imagined—to their security. The true condition of a country's freedom can best be seen by stripping away the legal jargon and focusing on the actual balance it has struck between liberty and security.

9. Koch and Peden, *Life and Selected Writings of Thomas Jefferson*, p. 321.

10. See Alan Dershowitz, *Supreme Injustice: How the High Court Hijacked Election 2000* (New York: Oxford University Press, 2001).

11. Mardy Grothe, *Oxymoronica* (New York: HarperCollins, 2004), p. 106.

12. Kaminski, *The Quotable Jefferson*, p. 391; see also p. 390.

13. Lester Cappon, ed., *The Adams-Jefferson Letters: The Complete Correspondence between Thomas Jefferson and Abigail and John Adams* (Chapel Hill: University of North Carolina Press, 1959), p. 279.

14. Alan Dershowitz, "Baseball's Speech Police," *New York Times*, February 2, 2000, p. A21.

15. For example, the Second Amendment—"A well regulated militia, being necessary to the security of a free state, the right of the people to keep and bear arms, shall not be infringed"—has been interpreted by the federal courts to include concepts of reasonableness. The 1968 gun control law (which was passed largely in response to the assassinations of John and Robert Kennedy and Martin Luther King Jr.) included provisions that prohibit certain individuals from buying or selling arms across state lines, including convicted felons, fugitives, those addicted to controlled substances, those under restraining orders, domestic violence offenders, and servicemen discharged dishonorably. Though challenged in the courts many times, the law has been repeatedly found to be consistent with the Second Amendment and the Equal Protection Clause of the Fourteenth Amendment (18 USCS § 922[g]; see *United States v. Emerson* [2001], *United States v. Darrington* [2003], *United States v. Chavarria* [2004], and so on.)

14 How Would Jefferson Strike the Balance between Freedom of Speech and Prevention of Terrorism?

1. John P. Kaminski, ed., *The Quotable Jefferson* (Princeton, NJ: Princeton University Press, 2006), pp. 164–166.

2. Ibid., p. 201.

3. Ibid., pp. 305–306.

4. Ibid., p. 201.

5. See the note regarding the letter to Benjamin Banneker, Philadelphia, August 30, 1791. Found in Kaminski, *The Quotable Jefferson*, p. 351.

6. See Alan Dershowitz, "Powell's Beau Ideal," *New Republic* (July 22, 1978), pp. 14–17. Also see Alan M. Dershowitz and Laura

Hanft, "Affirmative Action and the Harvard College Diversity-Discretion Model: Paradigm or Pretext?" 1 *Cardozo Law Review* 379 (1979): 386–400.

The incredible staying power of the "diversity-discretion" model is due as much to the model's marvelous ability to mask genuine institutional criteria, which cannot or will not be publicly articulated, as it is to any deep-seated belief in the value of diversity as an educational desideratum. . . . The raison d'etre for race-specific affirmative action programs has simply never been diversity for the sake of education. The checkered history of "diversity" demonstrates that it was designed largely as a cover to achieve other legally, morally, and politically controversial goals. . . . The "diversity-discretion" model thus subverts the ideals of responsibility and candor that are the hallmarks of any institution of learning in an open and democratic society.

7. Kaminski, *The Quotable Jefferson*, p. 390.

15 My View, as Influenced by Jefferson and the Experiences of Our Time

1. "Mitzvah goreret mitzvah, avaira goreret avaira," from the Mishna, *Pirkei Avot* 4:2.
2. As Griswold stated, "The line I would have to divide between opinions, to separate those the teaching of which shall be punishable, from those which may be taught with impunity. On the one side are all those things concerning which conscience dictates something. On the other all those things concerning which she dictates nothing." See Griswold's sermon in appendix B of this volume.
3. Quoted in Joyce Appleby and Terence Ball, eds., *Jefferson's Political Writings* (Cambridge, MA: Cambridge University Press, 1999), pp. 270–271.

INDEX

Page numbers in *italics* refer to illustrations.